D1996577

Virtual reality
Complete Self-Assessment Guide

The guidance in this Self-Assessment is based on Virtual reality best practices and standards in business process architecture, design and quality management. The guidance is also based on the professional judgment of the individual collaborators listed in the Acknowledgments.

Table of Contents

About The Art of Service

The Art of Service, Business Process Architects since 2000, is dedicated to helping stakeholders achieve excellence.

Defining, designing, creating, and implementing a process to solve a stakeholders challenge or meet an objective is the most valuable role... In EVERY group, company, organization and department.

Unless you're talking a one-time, single-use project, there should be a process. Whether that process is managed and implemented by humans, AI, or a combination of the two, it needs to be designed by someone with a complex enough perspective to ask the right questions.

Someone capable of asking the right questions and step back and say, 'What are we really trying to accomplish here? And is there a different way to look at it?'

With The Art of Service's Standard Requirements Self-Assessments, we empower people who can do just that — whether their title is marketer, entrepreneur, manager, salesperson, consultant, Business Process Manager, executive assistant, IT Manager, CIO etc... —they are the people who rule the future. They are people who watch the process as it happens, and ask the right questions to make the process work better.

Contact us when you need any support with this Self-Assessment and any help with templates, blue-prints and examples of standard documents you might need:

http://theartofservice.com
service@theartofservice.com

Acknowledgments

This checklist was developed under the auspices of The Art of Service, chaired by Gerardus Blokdyk.

Representatives from several client companies participated in the preparation of this Self-Assessment.

In addition, we are thankful for the design and printing services provided.

Included Resources - how to access

Included with your purchase of the book is the Virtual reality Self-Assessment Spreadsheet Dashboard which contains all questions and Self-Assessment areas and auto-generates insights, graphs, and project RACI planning - all with examples to get you started right away.

How? Simply send an email to
access@theartofservice.com
with this books' title in the subject to get the Virtual reality Self Assessment Tool right away.

You will receive the following contents with New and Updated specific criteria:

- The latest quick edition of the book in PDF
- The latest complete edition of the book in PDF, which criteria correspond to the criteria in...
- The Self-Assessment Excel Dashboard, and...
- Example pre-filled Self-Assessment Excel Dashboard to get familiar with results generation
- In-depth specific Checklists covering the topic
- Project management checklists and templates to assist with implementation

INCLUDES LIFETIME SELF ASSESSMENT UPDATES

Every self assessment comes with Lifetime Updates and Lifetime Free Updated Books. Lifetime Updates is an industry-first feature which allows you to receive verified self assessment updates, ensuring you always have the most accurate information at your fingertips.

Get it now- you will be glad you did - do it now, before you forget.

Send an email to **access@theartofservice.com** with this books' title in the subject to get the Virtual reality Self Assessment Tool right away.

Your feedback is invaluable to us

If you recently bought this book, we would love to hear from you! You can do this by writing a review on amazon (or the online store where you purchased this book) about your last purchase! As part of our continual service improvement process, we love to hear real client experiences and feedback.

How does it work?
To post a review on Amazon, just log in to your account and click on the Create Your Own Review button (under Customer Reviews) of the relevant product page. You can find examples of product reviews in Amazon. If you purchased from another online store, simply follow their procedures.

What happens when I submit my review?
Once you have submitted your review, send us an email at review@theartofservice.com with the link to your review so we can properly thank you for your feedback.

Purpose of this Self-Assessment

This Self-Assessment has been developed to improve understanding of the requirements and elements of Virtual reality, based on best practices and standards in business process architecture, design and quality management.

It is designed to allow for a rapid Self-Assessment to determine how closely existing management practices and procedures correspond to the elements of the Self-Assessment.

The criteria of requirements and elements of Virtual reality have been rephrased in the format of a Self-Assessment questionnaire, with a seven-criterion scoring system, as explained in this document.

In this format, even with limited background knowledge of

Virtual reality, a manager can quickly review existing operations to determine how they measure up to the standards. This in turn can serve as the starting point of a 'gap analysis' to identify management tools or system elements that might usefully be implemented in the organization to help improve overall performance.

How to use the Self-Assessment

On the following pages are a series of questions to identify to what extent your Virtual reality initiative is complete in comparison to the requirements set in standards.

To facilitate answering the questions, there is a space in front of each question to enter a score on a scale of '1' to '5'.

1 Strongly Disagree

2 Disagree

3 Neutral

4 Agree

5 Strongly Agree

Read the question and rate it with the following in front of mind:

**'In my belief,
the answer to this question is clearly defined'.**

There are two ways in which you can choose to interpret this statement;

1. how aware are you that the answer to the question is clearly defined
2. for more in-depth analysis you can choose to gather

evidence and confirm the answer to the question. This obviously will take more time, most Self-Assessment users opt for the first way to interpret the question and dig deeper later on based on the outcome of the overall Self-Assessment.

A score of '1' would mean that the answer is not clear at all, where a '5' would mean the answer is crystal clear and defined. Leave emtpy when the question is not applicable or you don't want to answer it, you can skip it without affecting your score. Write your score in the space provided.

After you have responded to all the appropriate statements in each section, compute your average score for that section, using the formula provided, and round to the nearest tenth. Then transfer to the corresponding spoke in the Virtual reality Scorecard on the second next page of the Self-Assessment.

Your completed Virtual reality Scorecard will give you a clear presentation of which Virtual reality areas need attention.

Virtual reality Scorecard Example

Example of how the finalized Scorecard can look like:

Virtual reality Scorecard

Your Scores:

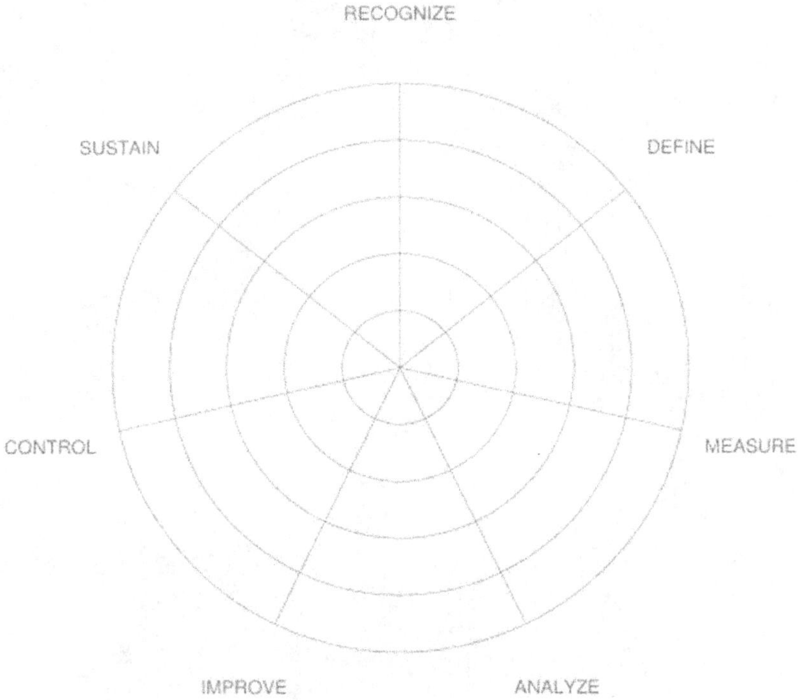

BEGINNING OF THE SELF-ASSESSMENT:

CRITERION #1: RECOGNIZE

INTENT: Be aware of the need for change. Recognize that there is an unfavorable variation, problem or symptom.

In my belief, the answer to this question is clearly defined:

5 Strongly Agree

4 Agree

3 Neutral

2 Disagree

1 Strongly Disagree

1. Who are your key stakeholders who need to sign off?
<--- Score

2. Can management personnel recognize the monetary benefit of Virtual reality?
<--- Score

3. As a sponsor, customer or management, how

important is it to meet goals, objectives?
<--- Score

4. What activities does the governance board need to consider?
<--- Score

5. What are your needs in relation to Virtual reality skills, labor, equipment, and markets?
<--- Score

6. What information do users need?
<--- Score

7. Are your goals realistic? Do you need to redefine your problem? Perhaps the problem has changed or maybe you have reached your goal and need to set a new one?
<--- Score

8. Will it solve real problems?
<--- Score

9. What training and capacity building actions are needed to implement proposed reforms?
<--- Score

10. Which information does the Virtual reality business case need to include?
<--- Score

11. Is it clear when you think of the day ahead of you what activities and tasks you need to complete?
<--- Score

12. How does it fit into your organizational needs and

tasks?
<--- Score

13. Have you identified your Virtual reality key performance indicators?
<--- Score

14. Do you need different information or graphics?
<--- Score

15. What are the timeframes required to resolve each of the issues/problems?
<--- Score

16. Will a response program recognize when a crisis occurs and provide some level of response?
<--- Score

17. Are there Virtual reality problems defined?
<--- Score

18. What is the problem or issue?
<--- Score

19. Does Virtual reality create potential expectations in other areas that need to be recognized and considered?
<--- Score

20. What should be considered when identifying available resources, constraints, and deadlines?
<--- Score

21. What situation(s) led to this Virtual reality Self Assessment?
<--- Score

22. What tools and technologies are needed for a custom Virtual reality project?
<--- Score

23. What problems are you facing and how do you consider Virtual reality will circumvent those obstacles?
<--- Score

24. Who else hopes to benefit from it?
<--- Score

25. How much are sponsors, customers, partners, stakeholders involved in Virtual reality? In other words, what are the risks, if Virtual reality does not deliver successfully?
<--- Score

26. Does your organization need more Virtual reality education?
<--- Score

27. What does Virtual reality success mean to the stakeholders?
<--- Score

28. Are you dealing with any of the same issues today as yesterday? What can you do about this?
<--- Score

29. How are you going to measure success?
<--- Score

30. Who defines the rules in relation to any given issue?

<--- Score

31. Is the need for organizational change recognized?
<--- Score

32. Are there any specific expectations or concerns about the Virtual reality team, Virtual reality itself?
<--- Score

33. What vendors make products that address the Virtual reality needs?
<--- Score

34. What is the smallest subset of the problem you can usefully solve?
<--- Score

35. How are the Virtual reality's objectives aligned to the group's overall stakeholder strategy?
<--- Score

36. For your Virtual reality project, identify and describe the business environment, is there more than one layer to the business environment?
<--- Score

37. What is the Virtual reality problem definition? What do you need to resolve?
<--- Score

38. How do you identify the kinds of information that you will need?
<--- Score

39. What are the stakeholder objectives to be achieved with Virtual reality?

<--- Score

40. Are there recognized Virtual reality problems?
<--- Score

41. What extra resources will you need?
<--- Score

42. Do you know what you need to know about Virtual reality?
<--- Score

43. How do you take a forward-looking perspective in identifying Virtual reality research related to market response and models?
<--- Score

44. What needs to be done?
<--- Score

45. Who needs to know about Virtual reality?
<--- Score

46. What prevents you from making the changes you know will make you a more effective Virtual reality leader?
<--- Score

47. What are the minority interests and what amount of minority interests can be recognized?
<--- Score

48. What are the expected benefits of Virtual reality to the stakeholder?
<--- Score

49. Think about the people you identified for your Virtual reality project and the project responsibilities you would assign to them, what kind of training do you think they would need to perform these responsibilities effectively?
<--- Score

50. Will new equipment/products be required to facilitate Virtual reality delivery, for example is new software needed?
<--- Score

51. Are controls defined to recognize and contain problems?
<--- Score

52. What would happen if Virtual reality weren't done?
<--- Score

53. What else needs to be measured?
<--- Score

54. Consider your own Virtual reality project, what types of organizational problems do you think might be causing or affecting your problem, based on the work done so far?
<--- Score

55. Are there any revenue recognition issues?
<--- Score

56. When a Virtual reality manager recognizes a problem, what options are available?
<--- Score

57. How do you assess your Virtual reality workforce

capability and capacity needs, including skills, competencies, and staffing levels?
<--- Score

58. Are employees recognized or rewarded for performance that demonstrates the highest levels of integrity?
<--- Score

59. Do you need to avoid or amend any Virtual reality activities?
<--- Score

60. Can virtual reality simulations be used as a research tool to study empathy, problems solving and perspective taking of educators?
<--- Score

61. Looking at each person individually – does every one have the qualities which are needed to work in this group?
<--- Score

62. Will Virtual reality deliverables need to be tested and, if so, by whom?
<--- Score

63. How can auditing be a preventative security measure?
<--- Score

64. What do you need to start doing?
<--- Score

65. To what extent would your organization benefit from being recognized as a award recipient?

<--- Score

66. Who needs what information?
<--- Score

67. Do you have/need 24-hour access to key personnel?
<--- Score

68. To what extent does each concerned units management team recognize Virtual reality as an effective investment?
<--- Score

69. Are problem definition and motivation clearly presented?
<--- Score

Add up total points for this section:
_____ = Total points for this section

Divided by: ______ (number of statements answered) = ______ Average score for this section

Transfer your score to the Virtual reality Index at the beginning of the Self-Assessment.

CRITERION #2: DEFINE:

INTENT: Formulate the stakeholder problem. Define the problem, needs and objectives.

In my belief, the answer to this question is clearly defined:

5 Strongly Agree

4 Agree

3 Neutral

2 Disagree

1 Strongly Disagree

1. Is there regularly 100% attendance at the team meetings? If not, have appointed substitutes attended to preserve cross-functionality and full representation?
<--- Score

2. Is Virtual reality required?
<--- Score

3. Is the scope of Virtual reality defined?
<--- Score

4. What is the scope?
<--- Score

5. When is/was the Virtual reality start date?
<--- Score

6. Has everyone on the team, including the team leaders, been properly trained?
<--- Score

7. The political context: who holds power?
<--- Score

8. What key stakeholder process output measure(s) does Virtual reality leverage and how?
<--- Score

9. Are different versions of process maps needed to account for the different types of inputs?
<--- Score

10. What are the Virtual reality use cases?
<--- Score

11. Who is gathering Virtual reality information?
<--- Score

12. How is the team tracking and documenting its work?
<--- Score

13. Is the team equipped with available and reliable resources?

<--- Score

14. What is in scope?
<--- Score

15. What baselines are required to be defined and managed?
<--- Score

16. How often are the team meetings?
<--- Score

17. How do you gather the stories?
<--- Score

18. Who are the Virtual reality improvement team members, including Management Leads and Coaches?
<--- Score

19. What are the core elements of the Virtual reality business case?
<--- Score

20. How will the Virtual reality team and the group measure complete success of Virtual reality?
<--- Score

21. What customer feedback methods were used to solicit their input?
<--- Score

22. If substitutes have been appointed, have they been briefed on the Virtual reality goals and received regular communications as to the progress to date?
<--- Score

23. What constraints exist that might impact the team?
<--- Score

24. Are accountability and ownership for Virtual reality clearly defined?
<--- Score

25. Are improvement team members fully trained on Virtual reality?
<--- Score

26. Where can you gather more information?
<--- Score

27. Have all basic functions of Virtual reality been defined?
<--- Score

28. Is there a critical path to deliver Virtual reality results?
<--- Score

29. How will variation in the actual durations of each activity be dealt with to ensure that the expected Virtual reality results are met?
<--- Score

30. Are task requirements clearly defined?
<--- Score

31. How do you manage unclear Virtual reality requirements?
<--- Score

32. Has anyone else (internal or external to the group) attempted to solve this problem or a similar one before? If so, what knowledge can be leveraged from these previous efforts?
<--- Score

33. Are required metrics defined, what are they?
<--- Score

34. Has a high-level 'as is' process map been completed, verified and validated?
<--- Score

35. What information should you gather?
<--- Score

36. What was the context?
<--- Score

37. Is there a clear Virtual reality case definition?
<--- Score

38. What happens if Virtual reality's scope changes?
<--- Score

39. Are there different segments of customers?
<--- Score

40. What are the tasks and definitions?
<--- Score

41. What defines best in class?
<--- Score

42. What is the definition of success?
<--- Score

43. Is it clearly defined in and to your organization what you do?
<--- Score

44. Is Virtual reality currently on schedule according to the plan?
<--- Score

45. Has a team charter been developed and communicated?
<--- Score

46. How did the Virtual reality manager receive input to the development of a Virtual reality improvement plan and the estimated completion dates/times of each activity?
<--- Score

47. What critical content must be communicated – who, what, when, where, and how?
<--- Score

48. How would you define the culture at your organization, how susceptible is it to Virtual reality changes?
<--- Score

49. What is in the scope and what is not in scope?
<--- Score

50. How do you gather requirements?
<--- Score

51. Are audit criteria, scope, frequency and methods defined?

<--- Score

52. How can the value of Virtual reality be defined?
<--- Score

53. Is the Virtual reality scope complete and appropriately sized?
<--- Score

54. How do you manage scope?
<--- Score

55. Scope of sensitive information?
<--- Score

56. Has a Virtual reality requirement not been met?
<--- Score

57. Is special Virtual reality user knowledge required?
<--- Score

58. How do you hand over Virtual reality context?
<--- Score

59. What are the Roles and Responsibilities for each team member and its leadership? Where is this documented?
<--- Score

60. When are meeting minutes sent out? Who is on the distribution list?
<--- Score

61. What is the context?
<--- Score

62. Have specific policy objectives been defined?
<--- Score

63. What Virtual reality requirements should be gathered?
<--- Score

64. Is the improvement team aware of the different versions of a process: what they think it is vs. what it actually is vs. what it should be vs. what it could be?
<--- Score

65. Is the current 'as is' process being followed? If not, what are the discrepancies?
<--- Score

66. What are the dynamics of the communication plan?
<--- Score

67. What would be the goal or target for a Virtual reality's improvement team?
<--- Score

68. Is data collected and displayed to better understand customer(s) critical needs and requirements.
<--- Score

69. What is out-of-scope initially?
<--- Score

70. Who defines (or who defined) the rules and roles?
<--- Score

71. Does the team have regular meetings?

<--- Score

72. Who is gathering information?
<--- Score

73. Has a project plan, Gantt chart, or similar been developed/completed?
<--- Score

74. In what way can you redefine the criteria of choice clients have in your category in your favor?
<--- Score

75. Are stakeholder processes mapped?
<--- Score

76. Has the improvement team collected the 'voice of the customer' (obtained feedback – qualitative and quantitative)?
<--- Score

77. Do you all define Virtual reality in the same way?
<--- Score

78. What are the rough order estimates on cost savings/opportunities that Virtual reality brings?
<--- Score

79. Has the Virtual reality work been fairly and/ or equitably divided and delegated among team members who are qualified and capable to perform the work? Has everyone contributed?
<--- Score

80. Are resources adequate for the scope?
<--- Score

81. How are consistent Virtual reality definitions important?
<--- Score

82. Are team charters developed?
<--- Score

83. Are approval levels defined for contracts and supplements to contracts?
<--- Score

84. Has your scope been defined?
<--- Score

85. Why are you doing Virtual reality and what is the scope?
<--- Score

86. Are customer(s) identified and segmented according to their different needs and requirements?
<--- Score

87. What scope to assess?
<--- Score

88. What is the worst case scenario?
<--- Score

89. Is there a completed, verified, and validated high-level 'as is' (not 'should be' or 'could be') stakeholder process map?
<--- Score

90. Is there a completed SIPOC representation, describing the Suppliers, Inputs, Process, Outputs, and

Customers?
<--- Score

91. Is there a Virtual reality management charter, including stakeholder case, problem and goal statements, scope, milestones, roles and responsibilities, communication plan?
<--- Score

92. What scope do you want your strategy to cover?
<--- Score

93. What Virtual reality services do you require?
<--- Score

94. Is the team adequately staffed with the desired cross-functionality? If not, what additional resources are available to the team?
<--- Score

95. Is the Virtual reality scope manageable?
<--- Score

96. Is the team formed and are team leaders (Coaches and Management Leads) assigned?
<--- Score

97. What information do you gather?
<--- Score

98. Are customers identified and high impact areas defined?
<--- Score

99. Is scope creep really all bad news?
<--- Score

100. Are there any constraints known that bear on the ability to perform Virtual reality work? How is the team addressing them?
<--- Score

101. What specifically is the problem? Where does it occur? When does it occur? What is its extent?
<--- Score

102. Has/have the customer(s) been identified?
<--- Score

103. Is Virtual reality linked to key stakeholder goals and objectives?
<--- Score

104. What is out of scope?
<--- Score

105. How do you manage changes in Virtual reality requirements?
<--- Score

106. How and when will the baselines be defined?
<--- Score

107. How do you think the partners involved in Virtual reality would have defined success?
<--- Score

108. Is full participation by members in regularly held team meetings guaranteed?
<--- Score

109. What is the scope of Virtual reality?

<--- Score

110. What are the compelling stakeholder reasons for embarking on Virtual reality?
<--- Score

111. How do you catch Virtual reality definition inconsistencies?
<--- Score

112. Have all of the relationships been defined properly?
<--- Score

113. What are the boundaries of the scope? What is in bounds and what is not? What is the start point? What is the stop point?
<--- Score

114. Do you have a Virtual reality success story or case study ready to tell and share?
<--- Score

115. What sort of initial information to gather?
<--- Score

116. Will a Virtual reality production readiness review be required?
<--- Score

117. Are roles and responsibilities formally defined?
<--- Score

118. How does the Virtual reality manager ensure against scope creep?
<--- Score

119. Has the direction changed at all during the course of Virtual reality? If so, when did it change and why?
<--- Score

120. Is the team sponsored by a champion or stakeholder leader?
<--- Score

121. What intelligence can you gather?
<--- Score

122. How do you keep key subject matter experts in the loop?
<--- Score

123. How was the 'as is' process map developed, reviewed, verified and validated?
<--- Score

124. Does the scope remain the same?
<--- Score

125. Is there any additional Virtual reality definition of success?
<--- Score

126. What are the record-keeping requirements of Virtual reality activities?
<--- Score

127. Have the customer needs been translated into specific, measurable requirements? How?
<--- Score

128. When is the estimated completion date?
<--- Score

129. What sources do you use to gather information for a Virtual reality study?
<--- Score

130. What are the Virtual reality tasks and definitions?
<--- Score

131. Do the problem and goal statements meet the SMART criteria (specific, measurable, attainable, relevant, and time-bound)?
<--- Score

132. How would you define Virtual reality leadership?
<--- Score

133. What is the scope of the Virtual reality effort?
<--- Score

134. What is the definition of Virtual reality excellence?
<--- Score

135. How have you defined all Virtual reality requirements first?
<--- Score

136. How do you gather Virtual reality requirements?
<--- Score

137. Will team members perform Virtual reality work when assigned and in a timely fashion?
<--- Score

138. What system do you use for gathering Virtual reality information?
<--- Score

139. Is a fully trained team formed, supported, and committed to work on the Virtual reality improvements?
<--- Score

140. Will team members regularly document their Virtual reality work?
<--- Score

Add up total points for this section:
_____ = Total points for this section

Divided by: ______ (number of statements answered) = ______ Average score for this section

Transfer your score to the Virtual reality Index at the beginning of the Self-Assessment.

CRITERION #3: MEASURE:

INTENT: Gather the correct data. Measure the current performance and evolution of the situation.

In my belief, the answer to this question is clearly defined:

5 Strongly Agree

4 Agree

3 Neutral

2 Disagree

1 Strongly Disagree

1. How can a Virtual reality test verify your ideas or assumptions?
<--- Score

2. Among the Virtual reality product and service cost to be estimated, which is considered hardest to estimate?
<--- Score

3. How do you know that any Virtual reality analysis is complete and comprehensive?
<--- Score

4. Are you able to realize any cost savings?
<--- Score

5. Have you included everything in your Virtual reality cost models?
<--- Score

6. How can you measure Virtual reality in a systematic way?
<--- Score

7. Was a business case (cost/benefit) developed?
<--- Score

8. Are you aware of what could cause a problem?
<--- Score

9. How can you manage cost down?
<--- Score

10. Who should receive measurement reports?
<--- Score

11. How will effects be measured?
<--- Score

12. What do you measure and why?
<--- Score

13. How will you measure success?
<--- Score

14. Are there measurements based on task performance?
<--- Score

15. Will Virtual reality have an impact on current business continuity, disaster recovery processes and/or infrastructure?
<--- Score

16. What are the uncertainties surrounding estimates of impact?
<--- Score

17. Have the concerns of stakeholders to help identify and define potential barriers been obtained and analyzed?
<--- Score

18. What methods are feasible and acceptable to estimate the impact of reforms?
<--- Score

19. When a disaster occurs, who gets priority?
<--- Score

20. Where can you go to verify the info?
<--- Score

21. What does losing customers cost your organization?
<--- Score

22. Does Virtual reality analysis isolate the fundamental causes of problems?
<--- Score

23. What relevant entities could be measured?
<--- Score

24. Are there any easy-to-implement alternatives to Virtual reality? Sometimes other solutions are available that do not require the cost implications of a full-blown project?
<--- Score

25. How are you verifying it?
<--- Score

26. How will you measure your Virtual reality effectiveness?
<--- Score

27. How are costs allocated?
<--- Score

28. What would be a real cause for concern?
<--- Score

29. What are you verifying?
<--- Score

30. Are the Virtual reality benefits worth its costs?
<--- Score

31. Are high impact defects defined and identified in the stakeholder process?
<--- Score

32. How do you verify Virtual reality completeness and accuracy?
<--- Score

33. Are the units of measure consistent?
<--- Score

34. How much does it cost?
<--- Score

35. Does the Virtual reality task fit the client's priorities?
<--- Score

36. How do you verify the authenticity of the data and information used?
<--- Score

37. What are the types and number of measures to use?
<--- Score

38. Do you have a flow diagram of what happens?
<--- Score

39. What harm might be caused?
<--- Score

40. Have you made assumptions about the shape of the future, particularly its impact on your customers and competitors?
<--- Score

41. What disadvantage does this cause for the user?
<--- Score

42. What can be used to verify compliance?
<--- Score

43. Are you taking your company in the direction of

better and revenue or cheaper and cost?
<--- Score

44. What are your key Virtual reality organizational performance measures, including key short and longer-term financial measures?
<--- Score

45. What is an unallowable cost?
<--- Score

46. What are the current costs of the Virtual reality process?
<--- Score

47. What are the operational costs after Virtual reality deployment?
<--- Score

48. What is the cost of rework?
<--- Score

49. When is Root Cause Analysis Required?
<--- Score

50. Is data collected on key measures that were identified?
<--- Score

51. Has a cost center been established?
<--- Score

52. The approach of traditional Virtual reality works for detail complexity but is focused on a systematic approach rather than an understanding of the nature of systems themselves, what approach will

permit your organization to deal with the kind of unpredictable emergent behaviors that dynamic complexity can introduce?
<--- Score

53. Is data collection planned and executed?
<--- Score

54. Which measures and indicators matter?
<--- Score

55. Do staff have the necessary skills to collect, analyze, and report data?
<--- Score

56. What is measured? Why?
<--- Score

57. How do you measure success?
<--- Score

58. Have you found any 'ground fruit' or 'low-hanging fruit' for immediate remedies to the gap in performance?
<--- Score

59. Have the types of risks that may impact Virtual reality been identified and analyzed?
<--- Score

60. How frequently do you verify your Virtual reality strategy?
<--- Score

61. How sensitive must the Virtual reality strategy be to cost?

<--- Score

62. What has the team done to assure the stability and accuracy of the measurement process?
<--- Score

63. What drives O&M cost?
<--- Score

64. Why do the measurements/indicators matter?
<--- Score

65. How do you measure variability?
<--- Score

66. Was a life-cycle cost analysis performed?
<--- Score

67. Are there competing Virtual reality priorities?
<--- Score

68. Is there an opportunity to verify requirements?
<--- Score

69. How do you aggregate measures across priorities?
<--- Score

70. What are the estimated costs of proposed changes?
<--- Score

71. Have design-to-cost goals been established?
<--- Score

72. How do you verify performance?
<--- Score

73. How frequently do you track Virtual reality measures?
<--- Score

74. What are the costs and benefits?
<--- Score

75. What measurements are possible, practicable and meaningful?
<--- Score

76. What are the Virtual reality key cost drivers?
<--- Score

77. Where is it measured?
<--- Score

78. How do you stay flexible and focused to recognize larger Virtual reality results?
<--- Score

79. Have all non-recommended alternatives been analyzed in sufficient detail?
<--- Score

80. What is your decision requirements diagram?
<--- Score

81. Do you have any cost Virtual reality limitation requirements?
<--- Score

82. What is your Virtual reality quality cost segregation study?
<--- Score

83. Are the measurements objective?
<--- Score

84. How do you verify and develop ideas and innovations?
<--- Score

85. What are the costs of reform?
<--- Score

86. Is a solid data collection plan established that includes measurement systems analysis?
<--- Score

87. What are the key input variables? What are the key process variables? What are the key output variables?
<--- Score

88. Did you tackle the cause or the symptom?
<--- Score

89. How do you measure lifecycle phases?
<--- Score

90. At what cost?
<--- Score

91. How can you reduce the costs of obtaining inputs?
<--- Score

92. What are your key Virtual reality indicators that you will measure, analyze and track?
<--- Score

93. Are losses documented, analyzed, and remedial

processes developed to prevent future losses?
<--- Score

94. What tests verify requirements?
<--- Score

95. Does a Virtual reality quantification method exist?
<--- Score

96. Have changes been properly/adequately analyzed for effect?
<--- Score

97. What could cause you to change course?
<--- Score

98. Do you aggressively reward and promote the people who have the biggest impact on creating excellent Virtual reality services/products?
<--- Score

99. What particular quality tools did the team find helpful in establishing measurements?
<--- Score

100. What evidence is there and what is measured?
<--- Score

101. Is key measure data collection planned and executed, process variation displayed and communicated and performance baselined?
<--- Score

102. How can you reduce costs?
<--- Score

103. How will measures be used to manage and adapt?
<--- Score

104. What is your cost benefit analysis?
<--- Score

105. What would it cost to replace your technology?
<--- Score

106. What causes innovation to fail or succeed in your organization?
<--- Score

107. Are process variation components displayed/ communicated using suitable charts, graphs, plots?
<--- Score

108. What causes extra work or rework?
<--- Score

109. How to cause the change?
<--- Score

110. Do you verify that corrective actions were taken?
<--- Score

111. What key measures identified indicate the performance of the stakeholder process?
<--- Score

112. Are indirect costs charged to the Virtual reality program?
<--- Score

113. How do you quantify and qualify impacts?

<--- Score

114. Is the cost worth the Virtual reality effort ?
<--- Score

115. What does a Test Case verify?
<--- Score

116. What are the agreed upon definitions of the high impact areas, defect(s), unit(s), and opportunities that will figure into the process capability metrics?
<--- Score

117. How do you control the overall costs of your work processes?
<--- Score

118. What are your primary costs, revenues, assets?
<--- Score

119. How do you do risk analysis of rare, cascading, catastrophic events?
<--- Score

120. What are allowable costs?
<--- Score

121. Is the solution cost-effective?
<--- Score

122. What are your customers expectations and measures?
<--- Score

123. How does cost-to-serve analysis help?
<--- Score

124. What is the total fixed cost?
<--- Score

125. How is progress measured?
<--- Score

126. What does verifying compliance entail?
<--- Score

127. What could cause delays in the schedule?
<--- Score

128. Are missed Virtual reality opportunities costing your organization money?
<--- Score

129. Does Virtual reality systematically track and analyze outcomes for accountability and quality improvement?
<--- Score

130. Is there a Performance Baseline?
<--- Score

131. How do you verify and validate the Virtual reality data?
<--- Score

132. When are costs are incurred?
<--- Score

133. Is the scope of Virtual reality cost analysis cost-effective?
<--- Score

134. What are the costs of delaying Virtual reality action?
<--- Score

135. Does Virtual reality analysis show the relationships among important Virtual reality factors?
<--- Score

136. What measurements are being captured?
<--- Score

137. Which costs should be taken into account?
<--- Score

138. Is it possible to estimate the impact of unanticipated complexity such as wrong or failed assumptions, feedback, etcetera on proposed reforms?
<--- Score

139. How will your organization measure success?
<--- Score

140. When should you bother with diagrams?
<--- Score

141. How do you focus on what is right -not who is right?
<--- Score

142. How is the value delivered by Virtual reality being measured?
<--- Score

143. How do you identify and analyze stakeholders and their interests?

<--- Score

144. Are actual costs in line with budgeted costs?
<--- Score

145. What causes investor action?
<--- Score

146. What data was collected (past, present, future/ ongoing)?
<--- Score

147. What does your operating model cost?
<--- Score

148. Why do you expend time and effort to implement measurement, for whom?
<--- Score

149. Who is involved in verifying compliance?
<--- Score

150. What potential environmental factors impact the Virtual reality effort?
<--- Score

151. Do you effectively measure and reward individual and team performance?
<--- Score

152. Can you do Virtual reality without complex (expensive) analysis?
<--- Score

153. What is the right balance of time and resources between investigation, analysis, and discussion and

dissemination?
<--- Score

154. Was a data collection plan established?
<--- Score

155. What causes mismanagement?
<--- Score

156. Is Process Variation Displayed/Communicated?
<--- Score

157. How do you measure efficient delivery of Virtual reality services?
<--- Score

158. How do you verify if Virtual reality is built right?
<--- Score

159. What charts has the team used to display the components of variation in the process?
<--- Score

160. What happens if cost savings do not materialize?
<--- Score

161. How do you prevent mis-estimating cost?
<--- Score

162. How will costs be allocated?
<--- Score

163. How is performance measured?
<--- Score

164. Has a cost benefit analysis been performed?

<--- Score

165. How do you verify the Virtual reality requirements quality?
<--- Score

166. How can you measure the performance?
<--- Score

167. Which stakeholder characteristics are analyzed?
<--- Score

168. Does your organization systematically track and analyze outcomes related for accountability and quality improvement?
<--- Score

169. How are measurements made?
<--- Score

170. How do your measurements capture actionable Virtual reality information for use in exceeding your customers expectations and securing your customers engagement?
<--- Score

171. What kind of analytics data will be gathered?
<--- Score

172. Are supply costs steady or fluctuating?
<--- Score

173. Can you measure the return on analysis?
<--- Score

174. Is long term and short term variability accounted

for?
<--- Score

175. How do you verify your resources?
<--- Score

176. What do people want to verify?
<--- Score

177. What are your operating costs?
<--- Score

178. Are key measures identified and agreed upon?
<--- Score

179. What is the total cost related to deploying Virtual reality, including any consulting or professional services?
<--- Score

180. How large is the gap between current performance and the customer-specified (goal) performance?
<--- Score

181. Who participated in the data collection for measurements?
<--- Score

182. Do the benefits outweigh the costs?
<--- Score

183. Is a follow-up focused external Virtual reality review required?
<--- Score

184. How will success or failure be measured?
<--- Score

Add up total points for this section:
_____ = Total points for this section

Divided by: ______ (number of statements answered) = ______ Average score for this section

Transfer your score to the Virtual reality Index at the beginning of the Self-Assessment.

CRITERION #4: ANALYZE:

INTENT: Analyze causes, assumptions and hypotheses.

In my belief, the answer to this question is clearly defined:

5 Strongly Agree

4 Agree

3 Neutral

2 Disagree

1 Strongly Disagree

1. Can you add value to the current Virtual reality decision-making process (largely qualitative) by incorporating uncertainty modeling (more quantitative)?
<--- Score

2. Was a detailed process map created to amplify critical steps of the 'as is' stakeholder process?
<--- Score

3. Were there any improvement opportunities identified from the process analysis?
<--- Score

4. What qualifications are needed?
<--- Score

5. Are Virtual reality changes recognized early enough to be approved through the regular process?
<--- Score

6. What do you need to qualify?
<--- Score

7. What are your best practices for minimizing Virtual reality project risk, while demonstrating incremental value and quick wins throughout the Virtual reality project lifecycle?
<--- Score

8. An organizationally feasible system request is one that considers the mission, goals and objectives of the organization, key questions are: is the Virtual reality solution request practical and will it solve a problem or take advantage of an opportunity to achieve company goals?
<--- Score

9. What controls do you have in place to protect data?
<--- Score

10. What are the best opportunities for value improvement?
<--- Score

11. Has data output been validated?

<--- Score

12. What is your organizations process which leads to recognition of value generation?
<--- Score

13. How many input/output points does it require?
<--- Score

14. Was a cause-and-effect diagram used to explore the different types of causes (or sources of variation)?
<--- Score

15. What is the output?
<--- Score

16. Do several people in different organizational units assist with the Virtual reality process?
<--- Score

17. What is the complexity of the output produced?
<--- Score

18. Have any additional benefits been identified that will result from closing all or most of the gaps?
<--- Score

19. What Virtual reality data do you gather or use now?
<--- Score

20. How is the data gathered?
<--- Score

21. How is Virtual reality data gathered?
<--- Score

22. What training and qualifications will you need?
<--- Score

23. How was the detailed process map generated, verified, and validated?
<--- Score

24. Were Pareto charts (or similar) used to portray the 'heavy hitters' (or key sources of variation)?
<--- Score

25. Is pre-qualification of suppliers carried out?
<--- Score

26. Are your outputs consistent?
<--- Score

27. Who will gather what data?
<--- Score

28. Are gaps between current performance and the goal performance identified?
<--- Score

29. Have you defined which data is gathered how?
<--- Score

30. A compounding model resolution with available relevant data can often provide insight towards a solution methodology; which Virtual reality models, tools and techniques are necessary?
<--- Score

31. Is the gap/opportunity displayed and communicated in financial terms?

<--- Score

32. How do mission and objectives affect the Virtual reality processes of your organization?
<--- Score

33. How does the organization define, manage, and improve its Virtual reality processes?
<--- Score

34. What information qualified as important?
<--- Score

35. Where is the data coming from to measure compliance?
<--- Score

36. Where can you get qualified talent today?
<--- Score

37. What quality tools were used to get through the analyze phase?
<--- Score

38. What qualifications and skills do you need?
<--- Score

39. What other jobs or tasks affect the performance of the steps in the Virtual reality process?
<--- Score

40. What are the necessary qualifications?
<--- Score

41. Do your leaders quickly bounce back from setbacks?

<--- Score

42. How are outputs preserved and protected?
<--- Score

43. Who gets your output?
<--- Score

44. Do you, as a leader, bounce back quickly from setbacks?
<--- Score

45. What are your outputs?
<--- Score

46. What tools were used to narrow the list of possible causes?
<--- Score

47. What are evaluation criteria for the output?
<--- Score

48. What are your key performance measures or indicators and in-process measures for the control and improvement of your Virtual reality processes?
<--- Score

49. What methods do you use to gather Virtual reality data?
<--- Score

50. Is the performance gap determined?
<--- Score

51. What are the disruptive Virtual reality technologies that enable your organization to radically change your

business processes?
<--- Score

52. What were the financial benefits resulting from any 'ground fruit or low-hanging fruit' (quick fixes)?
<--- Score

53. What are the personnel training and qualifications required?
<--- Score

54. Did any additional data need to be collected?
<--- Score

55. Do your employees have the opportunity to do what they do best everyday?
<--- Score

56. What is your organizations system for selecting qualified vendors?
<--- Score

57. How do you use Virtual reality data and information to support organizational decision making and innovation?
<--- Score

58. How do your work systems and key work processes relate to and capitalize on your core competencies?
<--- Score

59. What will drive Virtual reality change?
<--- Score

60. Record-keeping requirements flow from the

records needed as inputs, outputs, controls and for transformation of a Virtual reality process, are the records needed as inputs to the Virtual reality process available?
<--- Score

61. Think about some of the processes you undertake within your organization, which do you own?
<--- Score

62. What is the cost of poor quality as supported by the team's analysis?
<--- Score

63. Are all team members qualified for all tasks?
<--- Score

64. What does the data say about the performance of the stakeholder process?
<--- Score

65. Identify an operational issue in your organization, for example, could a particular task be done more quickly or more efficiently by Virtual reality?
<--- Score

66. What Virtual reality metrics are outputs of the process?
<--- Score

67. How difficult is it to qualify what Virtual reality ROI is?
<--- Score

68. What process should you select for improvement?
<--- Score

69. What successful thing are you doing today that may be blinding you to new growth opportunities?
<--- Score

70. How do you measure the operational performance of your key work systems and processes, including productivity, cycle time, and other appropriate measures of process effectiveness, efficiency, and innovation?
<--- Score

71. Have the problem and goal statements been updated to reflect the additional knowledge gained from the analyze phase?
<--- Score

72. What resources go in to get the desired output?
<--- Score

73. What kind of crime could a potential new hire have committed that would not only not disqualify him/her from being hired by your organization, but would actually indicate that he/she might be a particularly good fit?
<--- Score

74. What data is gathered?
<--- Score

75. How is the Virtual reality Value Stream Mapping managed?
<--- Score

76. What are your current levels and trends in key measures or indicators of Virtual reality product

and process performance that are important to and directly serve your customers? How do these results compare with the performance of your competitors and other organizations with similar offerings?
<--- Score

77. Do your contracts/agreements contain data security obligations?
<--- Score

78. Do staff qualifications match your project?
<--- Score

79. How is the way you as the leader think and process information affecting your organizational culture?
<--- Score

80. Is the final output clearly identified?
<--- Score

81. Should you invest in industry-recognized qualifications?
<--- Score

82. What qualifications do Virtual reality leaders need?
<--- Score

83. How do you promote understanding that opportunity for improvement is not criticism of the status quo, or the people who created the status quo?
<--- Score

84. What tools were used to generate the list of possible causes?
<--- Score

85. How do you implement and manage your work processes to ensure that they meet design requirements?
<--- Score

86. How has the Virtual reality data been gathered?
<--- Score

87. What conclusions were drawn from the team's data collection and analysis? How did the team reach these conclusions?
<--- Score

88. Where is Virtual reality data gathered?
<--- Score

89. What are the revised rough estimates of the financial savings/opportunity for Virtual reality improvements?
<--- Score

90. What other organizational variables, such as reward systems or communication systems, affect the performance of this Virtual reality process?
<--- Score

91. What are your current levels and trends in key Virtual reality measures or indicators of product and process performance that are important to and directly serve your customers?
<--- Score

92. What were the crucial 'moments of truth' on the process map?
<--- Score

93. Do you have the authority to produce the output?
<--- Score

94. What output to create?
<--- Score

95. How do you identify specific Virtual reality investment opportunities and emerging trends?
<--- Score

96. Who is involved with workflow mapping?
<--- Score

97. Who qualifies to gain access to data?
<--- Score

98. What did the team gain from developing a sub-process map?
<--- Score

99. Has an output goal been set?
<--- Score

100. What qualifications are necessary?
<--- Score

101. Is the suppliers process defined and controlled?
<--- Score

102. Were any designed experiments used to generate additional insight into the data analysis?
<--- Score

103. How do you define collaboration and team output?
<--- Score

104. What are your Virtual reality processes?
<--- Score

105. Is data and process analysis, root cause analysis and quantifying the gap/opportunity in place?
<--- Score

106. What qualifies as competition?
<--- Score

107. Is the Virtual reality process severely broken such that a re-design is necessary?
<--- Score

108. Think about the functions involved in your Virtual reality project, what processes flow from these functions?
<--- Score

109. Did any value-added analysis or 'lean thinking' take place to identify some of the gaps shown on the 'as is' process map?
<--- Score

110. What data do you need to collect?
<--- Score

111. Are all staff in core Virtual reality subjects Highly Qualified?
<--- Score

112. How often will data be collected for measures?
<--- Score

113. What is the Value Stream Mapping?

<--- Score

114. Is the required Virtual reality data gathered?
<--- Score

Add up total points for this section:
_____ = Total points for this section

Divided by: ______ (number of statements answered) = ______ Average score for this section

Transfer your score to the Virtual reality Index at the beginning of the Self-Assessment.

CRITERION #5: IMPROVE:

INTENT: Develop a practical solution. Innovate, establish and test the solution and to measure the results.

In my belief, the answer to this question is clearly defined:

5 Strongly Agree

4 Agree

3 Neutral

2 Disagree

1 Strongly Disagree

1. Explorations of the frontiers of Virtual reality will help you build influence, improve Virtual reality, optimize decision making, and sustain change, what is your approach?
<--- Score

2. What communications are necessary to support the implementation of the solution?
<--- Score

3. Which of the recognised risks out of all risks can be most likely transferred?
<--- Score

4. Have you identified breakpoints and/or risk tolerances that will trigger broad consideration of a potential need for intervention or modification of strategy?
<--- Score

5. What tools were used to tap into the creativity and encourage 'outside the box' thinking?
<--- Score

6. Were any criteria developed to assist the team in testing and evaluating potential solutions?
<--- Score

7. How do you manage and improve your Virtual reality work systems to deliver customer value and achieve organizational success and sustainability?
<--- Score

8. How do you keep improving Virtual reality?
<--- Score

9. Who will be responsible for making the decisions to include or exclude requested changes once Virtual reality is underway?
<--- Score

10. Are risk triggers captured?
<--- Score

11. Why improve in the first place?

<--- Score

12. For decision problems, how do you develop a decision statement?
<--- Score

13. What are the implications of the one critical Virtual reality decision 10 minutes, 10 months, and 10 years from now?
<--- Score

14. Do those selected for the Virtual reality team have a good general understanding of what Virtual reality is all about?
<--- Score

15. For estimation problems, how do you develop an estimation statement?
<--- Score

16. What does the 'should be' process map/design look like?
<--- Score

17. How do you define the solutions' scope?
<--- Score

18. How will the team or the process owner(s) monitor the implementation plan to see that it is working as intended?
<--- Score

19. How do you link measurement and risk?
<--- Score

20. What were the underlying assumptions on the

cost-benefit analysis?
<--- Score

21. Are improved process ('should be') maps modified based on pilot data and analysis?
<--- Score

22. Is a solution implementation plan established, including schedule/work breakdown structure, resources, risk management plan, cost/budget, and control plan?
<--- Score

23. How do you improve your likelihood of success ?
<--- Score

24. Will the controls trigger any other risks?
<--- Score

25. Who will be responsible for documenting the Virtual reality requirements in detail?
<--- Score

26. What lessons, if any, from a pilot were incorporated into the design of the full-scale solution?
<--- Score

27. Risk Identification: What are the possible risk events your organization faces in relation to Virtual reality?
<--- Score

28. Is the optimal solution selected based on testing and analysis?
<--- Score

29. Is supporting Virtual reality documentation required?
<--- Score

30. What needs improvement? Why?
<--- Score

31. How will you know when its improved?
<--- Score

32. Who are the people involved in developing and implementing Virtual reality?
<--- Score

33. Who controls key decisions that will be made?
<--- Score

34. What resources are required for the improvement efforts?
<--- Score

35. Do you cover the five essential competencies: Communication, Collaboration,Innovation, Adaptability, and Leadership that improve an organizations ability to leverage the new Virtual reality in a volatile global economy?
<--- Score

36. What practices helps your organization to develop its capacity to recognize patterns?
<--- Score

37. What went well, what should change, what can improve?
<--- Score

38. Is the solution technically practical?
<--- Score

39. Was a pilot designed for the proposed solution(s)?
<--- Score

40. Risk events: what are the things that could go wrong?
<--- Score

41. How do you measure risk?
<--- Score

42. How significant is the improvement in the eyes of the end user?
<--- Score

43. Does the goal represent a desired result that can be measured?
<--- Score

44. What attendant changes will need to be made to ensure that the solution is successful?
<--- Score

45. How can you improve Virtual reality?
<--- Score

46. Is a contingency plan established?
<--- Score

47. Are decisions made in a timely manner?
<--- Score

48. Is there a cost/benefit analysis of optimal solution(s)?

<--- Score

49. Is the implementation plan designed?
<--- Score

50. What improvements have been achieved?
<--- Score

51. What actually has to improve and by how much?
<--- Score

52. How risky is your organization?
<--- Score

53. What error proofing will be done to address some of the discrepancies observed in the 'as is' process?
<--- Score

54. What to do with the results or outcomes of measurements?
<--- Score

55. How does the solution remove the key sources of issues discovered in the analyze phase?
<--- Score

56. Is the measure of success for Virtual reality understandable to a variety of people?
<--- Score

57. How do you improve productivity?
<--- Score

58. What tools do you use once you have decided on a Virtual reality strategy and more importantly how do you choose?

<--- Score

59. Is pilot data collected and analyzed?
<--- Score

60. What tools were used to evaluate the potential solutions?
<--- Score

61. When you map the key players in your own work and the types/domains of relationships with them, which relationships do you find easy and which challenging, and why?
<--- Score

62. Was a Virtual reality charter developed?
<--- Score

63. How can skill-level changes improve Virtual reality?
<--- Score

64. Can you identify any significant risks or exposures to Virtual reality third- parties (vendors, service providers, alliance partners etc) that concern you?
<--- Score

65. How will you know that you have improved?
<--- Score

66. In the past few months, what is the smallest change you have made that has had the biggest positive result? What was it about that small change that produced the large return?
<--- Score

67. How are policy decisions made and where?
<--- Score

68. How will you measure the results?
<--- Score

69. How does the team improve its work?
<--- Score

70. Are there any constraints (technical, political, cultural, or otherwise) that would inhibit certain solutions?
<--- Score

71. How do you decide how much to remunerate an employee?
<--- Score

72. What is Virtual reality's impact on utilizing the best solution(s)?
<--- Score

73. How do you improve Virtual reality service perception, and satisfaction?
<--- Score

74. How do you go about comparing Virtual reality approaches/solutions?
<--- Score

75. What is the team's contingency plan for potential problems occurring in implementation?
<--- Score

76. Virtual reality risk decisions: whose call Is It?
<--- Score

77. What are your current levels and trends in key measures or indicators of workforce and leader development?
<--- Score

78. Are possible solutions generated and tested?
<--- Score

79. How will you know that a change is an improvement?
<--- Score

80. How will the group know that the solution worked?
<--- Score

81. What is the current status of development in virtual reality?
<--- Score

82. Who do you report Virtual reality results to?
<--- Score

83. What is the implementation plan?
<--- Score

84. What do you want to improve?
<--- Score

85. Does a good decision guarantee a good outcome?
<--- Score

86. What tools were most useful during the improve phase?
<--- Score

87. How did the team generate the list of possible solutions?
<--- Score

88. What is the risk?
<--- Score

89. Is there a high likelihood that any recommendations will achieve their intended results?
<--- Score

90. Are the best solutions selected?
<--- Score

91. What can you do to improve?
<--- Score

92. To what extent does management recognize Virtual reality as a tool to increase the results?
<--- Score

93. Is the scope clearly documented?
<--- Score

94. Who will be using the results of the measurement activities?
<--- Score

95. How do you measure improved Virtual reality service perception, and satisfaction?
<--- Score

96. How do you measure progress and evaluate training effectiveness?
<--- Score

97. What should a proof of concept or pilot accomplish?
<--- Score

98. If you could go back in time five years, what decision would you make differently? What is your best guess as to what decision you're making today you might regret five years from now?
<--- Score

99. Who controls the risk?
<--- Score

100. Do you combine technical expertise with business knowledge and Virtual reality Key topics include lifecycles, development approaches, requirements and how to make a business case?
<--- Score

101. Are you assessing Virtual reality and risk?
<--- Score

102. Are new and improved process ('should be') maps developed?
<--- Score

103. Who makes the Virtual reality decisions in your organization?
<--- Score

104. Risk factors: what are the characteristics of Virtual reality that make it risky?
<--- Score

105. What is the Virtual reality's sustainability risk?

<--- Score

106. Can the solution be designed and implemented within an acceptable time period?
<--- Score

107. How do the Virtual reality results compare with the performance of your competitors and other organizations with similar offerings?
<--- Score

108. What is the magnitude of the improvements?
<--- Score

109. At what point will vulnerability assessments be performed once Virtual reality is put into production (e.g., ongoing Risk Management after implementation)?
<--- Score

110. Describe the design of the pilot and what tests were conducted, if any?
<--- Score

111. How can you improve performance?
<--- Score

112. Is there a small-scale pilot for proposed improvement(s)? What conclusions were drawn from the outcomes of a pilot?
<--- Score

Add up total points for this section:
_____ = Total points for this section

Divided by: ______ (number of

statements answered) = ______
Average score for this section

Transfer your score to the Virtual reality Index at the beginning of the Self-Assessment.

CRITERION #6: CONTROL:

INTENT: Implement the practical solution. Maintain the performance and correct possible complications.

In my belief, the answer to this question is clearly defined:

5 Strongly Agree

4 Agree

3 Neutral

2 Disagree

1 Strongly Disagree

1. How do your controls stack up?
<--- Score

2. How do you establish and deploy modified action plans if circumstances require a shift in plans and rapid execution of new plans?
<--- Score

3. How do you select, collect, align, and integrate

Virtual reality data and information for tracking daily operations and overall organizational performance, including progress relative to strategic objectives and action plans?
<--- Score

4. What other areas of the group might benefit from the Virtual reality team's improvements, knowledge, and learning?
<--- Score

5. How do senior leaders actions reflect a commitment to the organizations Virtual reality values?
<--- Score

6. How might the group capture best practices and lessons learned so as to leverage improvements?
<--- Score

7. Can you adapt and adjust to changing Virtual reality situations?
<--- Score

8. Are pertinent alerts monitored, analyzed and distributed to appropriate personnel?
<--- Score

9. What is the control/monitoring plan?
<--- Score

10. What should the next improvement project be that is related to Virtual reality?
<--- Score

11. Against what alternative is success being

measured?
<--- Score

12. Are the planned controls working?
<--- Score

13. Are suggested corrective/restorative actions indicated on the response plan for known causes to problems that might surface?
<--- Score

14. Is there a recommended audit plan for routine surveillance inspections of Virtual reality's gains?
<--- Score

15. In the case of a Virtual reality project, the criteria for the audit derive from implementation objectives, an audit of a Virtual reality project involves assessing whether the recommendations outlined for implementation have been met, can you track that any Virtual reality project is implemented as planned, and is it working?
<--- Score

16. Implementation Planning: is a pilot needed to test the changes before a full roll out occurs?
<--- Score

17. What do your reports reflect?
<--- Score

18. You may have created your quality measures at a time when you lacked resources, technology wasn't up to the required standard, or low service levels were the industry norm. Have those circumstances changed?

<--- Score

19. Is a response plan in place for when the input, process, or output measures indicate an 'out-of-control' condition?
<--- Score

20. Where do ideas that reach policy makers and planners as proposals for Virtual reality strengthening and reform actually originate?
<--- Score

21. How do controls support value?
<--- Score

22. How will you measure your QA plan's effectiveness?
<--- Score

23. Act/Adjust: What Do you Need to Do Differently?
<--- Score

24. How will report readings be checked to effectively monitor performance?
<--- Score

25. Does job training on the documented procedures need to be part of the process team's education and training?
<--- Score

26. Is there a standardized process?
<--- Score

27. What can you control?
<--- Score

28. What other systems, operations, processes, and infrastructures (hiring practices, staffing, training, incentives/rewards, metrics/dashboards/scorecards, etc.) need updates, additions, changes, or deletions in order to facilitate knowledge transfer and improvements?
<--- Score

29. What adjustments to the strategies are needed?
<--- Score

30. What are the critical parameters to watch?
<--- Score

31. Does the response plan contain a definite closed loop continual improvement scheme (e.g., plan-do-check-act)?
<--- Score

32. How do you plan on providing proper recognition and disclosure of supporting companies?
<--- Score

33. Are you measuring, monitoring and predicting Virtual reality activities to optimize operations and profitability, and enhancing outcomes?
<--- Score

34. Will any special training be provided for results interpretation?
<--- Score

35. What is the recommended frequency of auditing?
<--- Score

36. Will your goals reflect your program budget?
<--- Score

37. Is knowledge gained on process shared and institutionalized?
<--- Score

38. Is there a transfer of ownership and knowledge to process owner and process team tasked with the responsibilities.
<--- Score

39. How widespread is its use?
<--- Score

40. What are the known security controls?
<--- Score

41. Have new or revised work instructions resulted?
<--- Score

42. Has the improved process and its steps been standardized?
<--- Score

43. Are new process steps, standards, and documentation ingrained into normal operations?
<--- Score

44. Do you monitor the Virtual reality decisions made and fine tune them as they evolve?
<--- Score

45. Is there a Virtual reality Communication plan covering who needs to get what information when?
<--- Score

46. Will existing staff require re-training, for example, to learn new business processes?
<--- Score

47. Can support from partners be adjusted?
<--- Score

48. Does the Virtual reality performance meet the customer's requirements?
<--- Score

49. Is the Virtual reality test/monitoring cost justified?
<--- Score

50. How is Virtual reality project cost planned, managed, monitored?
<--- Score

51. How do you plan for the cost of succession?
<--- Score

52. Does a troubleshooting guide exist or is it needed?
<--- Score

53. Are operating procedures consistent?
<--- Score

54. Are documented procedures clear and easy to follow for the operators?
<--- Score

55. What are your results for key measures or indicators of the accomplishment of your Virtual reality strategy and action plans, including building and strengthening core competencies?

<--- Score

56. What quality tools were useful in the control phase?
<--- Score

57. Is there documentation that will support the successful operation of the improvement?
<--- Score

58. How can you best use all of your knowledge repositories to enhance learning and sharing?
<--- Score

59. What are you attempting to measure/monitor?
<--- Score

60. Is new knowledge gained imbedded in the response plan?
<--- Score

61. Who is the Virtual reality process owner?
<--- Score

62. Who will be in control?
<--- Score

63. Who is going to spread your message?
<--- Score

64. Is reporting being used or needed?
<--- Score

65. How is change control managed?
<--- Score

66. What should you measure to verify efficiency gains?
<--- Score

67. Does Virtual reality appropriately measure and monitor risk?
<--- Score

68. Who controls critical resources?
<--- Score

69. How will new or emerging customer needs/requirements be checked/communicated to orient the process toward meeting the new specifications and continually reducing variation?
<--- Score

70. Is a response plan established and deployed?
<--- Score

71. How do you monitor usage and cost?
<--- Score

72. Is there a documented and implemented monitoring plan?
<--- Score

73. How will the day-to-day responsibilities for monitoring and continual improvement be transferred from the improvement team to the process owner?
<--- Score

74. Are there documented procedures?
<--- Score

75. How will the process owner verify improvement in present and future sigma levels, process capabilities?
<--- Score

76. Will the team be available to assist members in planning investigations?
<--- Score

77. Do you monitor the effectiveness of your Virtual reality activities?
<--- Score

78. What do you measure to verify effectiveness gains?
<--- Score

79. Are controls in place and consistently applied?
<--- Score

80. Who sets the Virtual reality standards?
<--- Score

81. Are the planned controls in place?
<--- Score

82. How will input, process, and output variables be checked to detect for sub-optimal conditions?
<--- Score

83. Is there an action plan in case of emergencies?
<--- Score

84. How will Virtual reality decisions be made and monitored?
<--- Score

85. How do you encourage people to take control and responsibility?
<--- Score

86. How do you spread information?
<--- Score

87. How likely is the current Virtual reality plan to come in on schedule or on budget?
<--- Score

88. Is there a control plan in place for sustaining improvements (short and long-term)?
<--- Score

89. The case for social organization in computer-based teaching: Do employees learn more deeply when they interact with animated pedagogical agents?
<--- Score

90. What do you stand for--and what are you against?
<--- Score

91. How will the process owner and team be able to hold the gains?
<--- Score

92. Do the Virtual reality decisions you make today help people and the planet tomorrow?
<--- Score

93. What is the best design framework for Virtual reality organization now that, in a post industrial-age if the top-down, command and control model is no longer relevant?

<--- Score

94. What is your theory of human motivation, and how does your compensation plan fit with that view?
<--- Score

95. What are the key elements of your Virtual reality performance improvement system, including your evaluation, organizational learning, and innovation processes?
<--- Score

96. How will virtual reality, machine learning, blockchain, and many other emerging technologies change the role of the supply and maintenance professional?
<--- Score

97. Has the Virtual reality value of standards been quantified?
<--- Score

98. Can virtual reality support abstract concept learning?
<--- Score

99. Who has control over resources?
<--- Score

100. What key inputs and outputs are being measured on an ongoing basis?
<--- Score

Add up total points for this section:
_____ = Total points for this section

Divided by: ______ (number of statements answered) = ______ Average score for this section

Transfer your score to the Virtual reality Index at the beginning of the Self-Assessment.

CRITERION #7: SUSTAIN:

INTENT: Retain the benefits.

In my belief, the answer to this question is clearly defined:

5 Strongly Agree

4 Agree

3 Neutral

2 Disagree

1 Strongly Disagree

1. If you had to leave your organization for a year and the only communication you could have with employees/colleagues was a single paragraph, what would you write?
<--- Score

2. To whom do you add value?
<--- Score

3. What are the barriers to increased Virtual reality production?

<--- Score

4. What knowledge, skills and characteristics mark a good Virtual reality project manager?
<--- Score

5. Can the schedule be done in the given time?
<--- Score

6. What is the overall business strategy?
<--- Score

7. What are the gaps in your knowledge and experience?
<--- Score

8. If you do not follow, then how to lead?
<--- Score

9. How will you ensure you get what you expected?
<--- Score

10. How do you make it meaningful in connecting Virtual reality with what users do day-to-day?
<--- Score

11. Are you using a design thinking approach and integrating Innovation, Virtual reality Experience, and Brand Value?
<--- Score

12. How will you motivate the stakeholders with the least vested interest?
<--- Score

13. What new services of functionality will be

implemented next with Virtual reality ?
<--- Score

14. Is a Virtual reality team work effort in place?
<--- Score

15. How is augmented reality different from virtual reality?
<--- Score

16. Are you relevant? Will you be relevant five years from now? Ten?
<--- Score

17. What role does communication play in the success or failure of a Virtual reality project?
<--- Score

18. What is the big Virtual reality idea?
<--- Score

19. How will you know that the Virtual reality project has been successful?
<--- Score

20. What unique value proposition (UVP) do you offer?
<--- Score

21. What are strategies for increasing support and reducing opposition?
<--- Score

22. Is your strategy driving your strategy? Or is the way in which you allocate resources driving your strategy?
<--- Score

23. How do you proactively clarify deliverables and Virtual reality quality expectations?
<--- Score

24. How do you transition from the baseline to the target?
<--- Score

25. Do you have the right capabilities and capacities?
<--- Score

26. Are assumptions made in Virtual reality stated explicitly?
<--- Score

27. Whose voice (department, ethnic group, women, older workers, etc) might you have missed hearing from in your company, and how might you amplify this voice to create positive momentum for your business?
<--- Score

28. Who uses your product in ways you never expected?
<--- Score

29. What are internal and external Virtual reality relations?
<--- Score

30. Were lessons learned captured and communicated?
<--- Score

31. If you were responsible for initiating and

implementing major changes in your organization, what steps might you take to ensure acceptance of those changes?
<--- Score

32. Is your basic point ______ or ______?
<--- Score

33. What is an unauthorized commitment?
<--- Score

34. How do you engage the workforce, in addition to satisfying them?
<--- Score

35. How do you maintain Virtual reality's Integrity?
<--- Score

36. Are there any activities that you can take off your to do list?
<--- Score

37. Can you maintain your growth without detracting from the factors that have contributed to your success?
<--- Score

38. How do you keep the momentum going?
<--- Score

39. Is Virtual reality realistic, or are you setting yourself up for failure?
<--- Score

40. Who are your customers?
<--- Score

41. Why will customers want to buy your organizations products/services?
<--- Score

42. How do senior leaders deploy your organizations vision and values through your leadership system, to the workforce, to key suppliers and partners, and to customers and other stakeholders, as appropriate?
<--- Score

43. Who do you want your customers to become?
<--- Score

44. If you weren't already in this business, would you enter it today? And if not, what are you going to do about it?
<--- Score

45. What did you miss in the interview for the worst hire you ever made?
<--- Score

46. How do you deal with Virtual reality changes?
<--- Score

47. Is it economical; do you have the time and money?
<--- Score

48. Is maximizing Virtual reality protection the same as minimizing Virtual reality loss?
<--- Score

49. Operational - will it work?
<--- Score

50. How can you become the company that would put you out of business?
<--- Score

51. Who will be responsible for deciding whether Virtual reality goes ahead or not after the initial investigations?
<--- Score

52. Are you making progress, and are you making progress as Virtual reality leaders?
<--- Score

53. Who else should you help?
<--- Score

54. Who is responsible for errors?
<--- Score

55. Who will provide the final approval of Virtual reality deliverables?
<--- Score

56. What counts that you are not counting?
<--- Score

57. How likely is it that a customer would recommend your company to a friend or colleague?
<--- Score

58. What is the overall talent health of your organization as a whole at senior levels, and for each organization reporting to a member of the Senior Leadership Team?
<--- Score

59. What is the range of capabilities?
<--- Score

60. What is your competitive advantage?
<--- Score

61. Marketing budgets are tighter, consumers are more skeptical, and social media has changed forever the way we talk about Virtual reality, how do you gain traction?
<--- Score

62. What is a feasible sequencing of reform initiatives over time?
<--- Score

63. What trouble can you get into?
<--- Score

64. How do you assess the Virtual reality pitfalls that are inherent in implementing it?
<--- Score

65. What is the recommended frequency of auditing?
<--- Score

66. What are you trying to prove to yourself, and how might it be hijacking your life and business success?
<--- Score

67. How do you lead with Virtual reality in mind?
<--- Score

68. Think of your Virtual reality project, what are the main functions?
<--- Score

69. What have been your experiences in defining long range Virtual reality goals?
<--- Score

70. How important is Virtual reality to the user organizations mission?
<--- Score

71. What information is critical to your organization that your executives are ignoring?
<--- Score

72. Can you break it down?
<--- Score

73. How do you manage Virtual reality Knowledge Management (KM)?
<--- Score

74. How long will it take to change?
<--- Score

75. Is the Virtual reality organization completing tasks effectively and efficiently?
<--- Score

76. Do you say no to customers for no reason?
<--- Score

77. Is there any reason to believe the opposite of my current belief?
<--- Score

78. Virtual reality: what are the differences and similarities?

<--- Score

79. Have benefits been optimized with all key stakeholders?
<--- Score

80. What are the key enablers to make this Virtual reality move?
<--- Score

81. What was the last experiment you ran?
<--- Score

82. What one word do you want to own in the minds of your customers, employees, and partners?
<--- Score

83. What are the potential basics of Virtual reality fraud?
<--- Score

84. Would you rather sell to knowledgeable and informed customers or to uninformed customers?
<--- Score

85. What is the craziest thing you can do?
<--- Score

86. Are you / should you be revolutionary or evolutionary?
<--- Score

87. What are the essentials of internal Virtual reality management?
<--- Score

88. Is there any existing Virtual reality governance structure?
<--- Score

89. Which functions and people interact with the supplier and or customer?
<--- Score

90. Are you satisfied with your current role? If not, what is missing from it?
<--- Score

91. What would you recommend your friend do if he/ she were facing this dilemma?
<--- Score

92. What are the usability implications of Virtual reality actions?
<--- Score

93. If you find that you havent accomplished one of the goals for one of the steps of the Virtual reality strategy, what will you do to fix it?
<--- Score

94. What is the future of virtual reality and immersive 3D environments?
<--- Score

95. If there were zero limitations, what would you do differently?
<--- Score

96. What are the long-term Virtual reality goals?
<--- Score

97. What is it like to work for you?
<--- Score

98. What is effective Virtual reality?
<--- Score

99. Why do and why don't your customers like your organization?
<--- Score

100. If you got fired and a new hire took your place, what would she do different?
<--- Score

101. Which models, tools and techniques are necessary?
<--- Score

102. How do you track customer value, profitability or financial return, organizational success, and sustainability?
<--- Score

103. What may be the consequences for the performance of an organization if all stakeholders are not consulted regarding Virtual reality?
<--- Score

104. Who will determine interim and final deadlines?
<--- Score

105. Do you think you know, or do you know you know ?
<--- Score

106. Where can you break convention?

<--- Score

107. What is your question? Why?
<--- Score

108. What happens if you do not have enough funding?
<--- Score

109. Are your responses positive or negative?
<--- Score

110. Did your employees make progress today?
<--- Score

111. How does the effectiveness of this enhancement compare to other approaches?
<--- Score

112. How do you create buy-in?
<--- Score

113. Are you maintaining a past–present–future perspective throughout the Virtual reality discussion?
<--- Score

114. What are the rules and assumptions your industry operates under? What if the opposite were true?
<--- Score

115. What have you done to protect your business from competitive encroachment?
<--- Score

116. If your customer were your grandmother, would you tell her to buy what you're selling?

<--- Score

117. What do you mean by Virtual Reality (VR), Mixed Reality (MR) and Augmented Reality (AR)?
<--- Score

118. What is your formula for success in Virtual reality ?
<--- Score

119. Political -is anyone trying to undermine this project?
<--- Score

120. When information truly is ubiquitous, when reach and connectivity are completely global, when computing resources are infinite, and when a whole new set of impossibilities are not only possible, but happening, what will that do to your business?
<--- Score

121. How do you know if you are successful?
<--- Score

122. How do you govern and fulfill your societal responsibilities?
<--- Score

123. How will you buy Augmented Reality, Virtual Reality, 360 Video advertising formats?
<--- Score

124. How will you insure seamless interoperability of Virtual reality moving forward?
<--- Score

125. How do you go about securing Virtual reality?
<--- Score

126. What are the challenges?
<--- Score

127. Can you do all this work?
<--- Score

128. Who do you think the world wants your organization to be?
<--- Score

129. What is your BATNA (best alternative to a negotiated agreement)?
<--- Score

130. What are the success criteria that will indicate that Virtual reality objectives have been met and the benefits delivered?
<--- Score

131. How do you foster the skills, knowledge, talents, attributes, and characteristics you want to have?
<--- Score

132. What types of applications are best suited for current virtual reality technology?
<--- Score

133. Whom among your colleagues do you trust, and for what?
<--- Score

134. What will be the consequences to the stakeholder (financial, reputation etc) if Virtual reality

does not go ahead or fails to deliver the objectives?
<--- Score

135. What are the key differences between augmented reality and virtual reality?
<--- Score

136. What threat is Virtual reality addressing?
<--- Score

137. How can you incorporate support to ensure safe and effective use of Virtual reality into the services that you provide?
<--- Score

138. Have new benefits been realized?
<--- Score

139. Do you feel that more should be done in the Virtual reality area?
<--- Score

140. Is a Virtual reality breakthrough on the horizon?
<--- Score

141. What is the funding source for this project?
<--- Score

142. Is there a work around that you can use?
<--- Score

143. How do you accomplish your long range Virtual reality goals?
<--- Score

144. What is something you believe that nearly no one

agrees with you on?
<--- Score

145. Who is responsible for ensuring appropriate resources (time, people and money) are allocated to Virtual reality?
<--- Score

146. If your company went out of business tomorrow, would anyone who doesn't get a paycheck here care?
<--- Score

147. Who is the main stakeholder, with ultimate responsibility for driving Virtual reality forward?
<--- Score

148. What management system can you use to leverage the Virtual reality experience, ideas, and concerns of the people closest to the work to be done?
<--- Score

149. What are your personal philosophies regarding Virtual reality and how do they influence your work?
<--- Score

150. Instead of going to current contacts for new ideas, what if you reconnected with dormant contacts--the people you used to know? If you were going reactivate a dormant tie, who would it be?
<--- Score

151. Who is responsible for Virtual reality?
<--- Score

152. Are new benefits received and understood?

<--- Score

153. How do you provide a safe environment -physically and emotionally?
<--- Score

154. What could happen if you do not do it?
<--- Score

155. Has implementation been effective in reaching specified objectives so far?
<--- Score

156. What is the relationship between Augmented Reality (AR) and Virtual Reality (VR)?
<--- Score

157. Augmented and virtual reality: where is the educational value?
<--- Score

158. Who are four people whose careers you have enhanced?
<--- Score

159. What should you stop doing?
<--- Score

160. In the past year, what have you done (or could you have done) to increase the accurate perception of your company/brand as ethical and honest?
<--- Score

161. Ask yourself: how would you do this work if you only had one staff member to do it?
<--- Score

162. What are the top 3 things at the forefront of your Virtual reality agendas for the next 3 years?
<--- Score

163. What happens when a new employee joins the organization?
<--- Score

164. What does your signature ensure?
<--- Score

165. Do you have the right people on the bus?
<--- Score

166. What is the kind of project structure that would be appropriate for your Virtual reality project, should it be formal and complex, or can it be less formal and relatively simple?
<--- Score

167. What potential megatrends could make your business model obsolete?
<--- Score

168. Why is Virtual reality important for you now?
<--- Score

169. In a project to restructure Virtual reality outcomes, which stakeholders would you involve?
<--- Score

170. Which Virtual reality goals are the most important?
<--- Score

171. What current systems have to be understood and/or changed?
<--- Score

172. What happens at your organization when people fail?
<--- Score

173. How much contingency will be available in the budget?
<--- Score

174. How do you cross-sell and up-sell your Virtual reality success?
<--- Score

175. What is the purpose of Virtual reality in relation to the mission?
<--- Score

176. How do you stay inspired?
<--- Score

177. What you are going to do to affect the numbers?
<--- Score

178. How is implementation research currently incorporated into each of your goals?
<--- Score

179. Who have you, as a company, historically been when you've been at your best?
<--- Score

180. What would have to be true for the option on the table to be the best possible choice?

<--- Score

181. What is the estimated value of the project?
<--- Score

182. Who are the key stakeholders?
<--- Score

183. If you had to rebuild your organization without any traditional competitive advantages (i.e., no killer technology, promising research, innovative product/ service delivery model, etcetera), how would your people have to approach their work and collaborate together in order to create the necessary conditions for success?
<--- Score

184. In retrospect, of the projects that you pulled the plug on, what percent do you wish had been allowed to keep going, and what percent do you wish had ended earlier?
<--- Score

185. Is the impact that Virtual reality has shown?
<--- Score

186. How do you ensure that implementations of Virtual reality products are done in a way that ensures safety?
<--- Score

187. Do you have enough freaky customers in your portfolio pushing you to the limit day in and day out?
<--- Score

188. How can you become more high-tech but still be

high touch?
<--- Score

189. What projects are going on in the organization today, and what resources are those projects using from the resource pools?
<--- Score

190. How do customers see your organization?
<--- Score

191. What are your most important goals for the strategic Virtual reality objectives?
<--- Score

192. Do Virtual reality rules make a reasonable demand on a users capabilities?
<--- Score

193. How do you keep records, of what?
<--- Score

194. What is the source of the strategies for Virtual reality strengthening and reform?
<--- Score

195. How do you foster innovation?
<--- Score

196. Who is on the team?
<--- Score

197. Are you paying enough attention to the partners your company depends on to succeed?
<--- Score

198. What is your Virtual reality strategy?
<--- Score

199. What relationships among Virtual reality trends do you perceive?
<--- Score

200. Are the criteria for selecting recommendations stated?
<--- Score

201. How does Virtual reality integrate with other stakeholder initiatives?
<--- Score

202. Do you think Virtual reality accomplishes the goals you expect it to accomplish?
<--- Score

203. What trophy do you want on your mantle?
<--- Score

204. What goals did you miss?
<--- Score

205. Is Virtual reality dependent on the successful delivery of a current project?
<--- Score

206. At what moment would you think; Will I get fired?
<--- Score

207. What are the short and long-term Virtual reality goals?
<--- Score

208. Do you see more potential in people than they do in themselves?
<--- Score

209. Do you know what you are doing? And who do you call if you don't?
<--- Score

210. Are all key stakeholders present at all Structured Walkthroughs?
<--- Score

211. Can virtual reality support vocational training?
<--- Score

212. How do you set Virtual reality stretch targets and how do you get people to not only participate in setting these stretch targets but also that they strive to achieve these?
<--- Score

213. What do we do when new problems arise?
<--- Score

214. Which types of advertising will you buy in Augmented Reality, Virtual Reality, 360 Video?
<--- Score

215. Who will manage the integration of tools?
<--- Score

216. How do you determine the key elements that affect Virtual reality workforce satisfaction, how are these elements determined for different workforce groups and segments?

<--- Score

217. Who, on the executive team or the board, has spoken to a customer recently?
<--- Score

218. What stupid rule would you most like to kill?
<--- Score

219. What must you excel at?
<--- Score

220. Are you changing as fast as the world around you?
<--- Score

221. Why should people listen to you?
<--- Score

222. Are the assumptions believable and achievable?
<--- Score

223. How can you negotiate Virtual reality successfully with a stubborn boss, an irate client, or a deceitful coworker?
<--- Score

224. What are you challenging?
<--- Score

225. Why is it important to have senior management support for a Virtual reality project?
<--- Score

226. How do you listen to customers to obtain actionable information?

<--- Score

227. Why not do Virtual reality?
<--- Score

228. What business benefits will Virtual reality goals deliver if achieved?
<--- Score

229. Can virtual reality help deliver the goods?
<--- Score

230. Human futures: BCI cloudmind fulfillment or virtual reality couch potato?
<--- Score

231. What are the business goals Virtual reality is aiming to achieve?
<--- Score

232. Will it be accepted by users?
<--- Score

233. Which individuals, teams or departments will be involved in Virtual reality?
<--- Score

234. What Virtual reality skills are most important?
<--- Score

235. Which possibilities do augmented and virtual reality offer in psychotherapy?
<--- Score

236. How are you doing compared to your industry?
<--- Score

237. Will there be any necessary staff changes (redundancies or new hires)?
<--- Score

238. Why should you adopt a Virtual reality framework?
<--- Score

239. What are specific Virtual reality rules to follow?
<--- Score

240. What are current Virtual reality paradigms?
<--- Score

241. Do you have past Virtual reality successes?
<--- Score

242. How much does Virtual reality help?
<--- Score

243. Do you know who is a friend or a foe?
<--- Score

244. What Virtual reality modifications can you make work for you?
<--- Score

245. Who do we want your customers to become?
<--- Score

246. If no one would ever find out about your accomplishments, how would you lead differently?
<--- Score

247. Do you have an implicit bias for capital

investments over people investments?
<--- Score

Add up total points for this section:
_____ = Total points for this section

Divided by: ______ (number of statements answered) = ______ Average score for this section

Transfer your score to the Virtual reality Index at the beginning of the Self-Assessment.

Virtual reality and Managing Projects, Criteria for Project Managers:

1.0 Initiating Process Group: Virtual reality

1. What must be done?

2. Are the Virtual reality project team and stakeholders meeting regularly and using a meeting agenda and taking notes to accurately document what is being covered and what happened in the weekly meetings?

3. Will the Virtual reality project meet the client requirements, and will it achieve the business success criteria that justified doing the Virtual reality project in the first place?

4. Although the Virtual reality project manager does not directly manage procurement and contracting activities, who does manage procurement and contracting activities in your organization then if not the PM?

5. How to control and approve each phase?

6. What is the NEXT thing to do?

7. What are the pressing issues of the hour?

8. Do you know the roles & responsibilities required for this Virtual reality project?

9. Where must it be done?

10. The process to Manage Stakeholders is part of which process group?

11. Specific - is the objective clear in terms of what, how, when, and where the situation will be changed?

12. Who are the Virtual reality project stakeholders?

13. How will you know you did it?

14. What communication items need improvement?

15. Are you certain deliverables are properly completed and meet quality standards?

16. Just how important is your work to the overall success of the Virtual reality project?

17. What will you do to minimize the impact should a risk event occur?

18. What were the challenges that you encountered during the execution of a previous Virtual reality project that you would not want to repeat?

19. Were escalated issues resolved promptly?

20. Do you know all the stakeholders impacted by the Virtual reality project and what needs are?

1.1 Project Charter: Virtual reality

21. What are you striving to accomplish (measurable goal(s))?

22. Name and describe the elements that deal with providing the detail?

23. How do you manage integration?

24. What is the business need?

25. Fit with other Products Compliments – Cannibalizes?

26. What goes into your Virtual reality project Charter?

27. What does it need to do?

28. Who is the sponsor?

29. Why the improvements?

30. Why is it important?

31. What outcome, in measureable terms, are you hoping to accomplish?

32. How will you learn more about the process or system you are trying to improve?

33. Assumptions: what factors, for planning purposes, are you considering to be true?

34. What are some examples of a business case?

35. Why Outsource?

36. Does the Virtual reality project need to consider any special capacity or capability issues?

37. When?

38. Is time of the essence?

39. How much?

40. Are you building in-house ?

1.2 Stakeholder Register: Virtual reality

41. Who are the stakeholders?

42. Who is managing stakeholder engagement?

43. How should employers make voices heard?

44. How much influence do they have on the Virtual reality project?

45. What are the major Virtual reality project milestones requiring communications or providing communications opportunities?

46. Is your organization ready for change?

47. Who wants to talk about Security?

48. How will reports be created?

49. What is the power of the stakeholder?

50. How big is the gap?

51. What & Why?

52. What opportunities exist to provide communications?

1.3 Stakeholder Analysis Matrix: Virtual reality

53. How will the Virtual reality project benefit them?

54. Seasonality, weather effects?

55. Cultural, attitudinal, behavioural?

56. What do people from other organizations see as your strengths?

57. Market demand?

58. What can the stakeholder prevent from happening?

59. If the baseline is now, and if its improved it will be better than now?

60. Who will be affected by the Virtual reality project?

61. Who has not been involved up to now and should have been?

62. Insurmountable weaknesses?

63. Has there been a similar initiative in the region?

64. Who is influential in the Virtual reality project area (both thematic and geographic areas)?

65. New USPs?

66. Morale, commitment, leadership?

67. Guiding question: what is the issue at stake?

68. How can you counter negative efforts?

69. Accreditations, etc?

70. How are the threatened Virtual reality project targets being used?

71. What do you Evaluate?

2.0 Planning Process Group: Virtual reality

72. Did the program design/ implementation strategy adequately address the planning stage necessary to set up structures, hire staff etc.?

73. Professionals want to know what is expected from them; what are the deliverables?

74. Are there efficient coordination mechanisms to avoid overloading the counterparts, participating stakeholders?

75. How can you tell when you are done?

76. Have operating capacities been created and/or reinforced in partners?

77. Are the follow-up indicators relevant and do they meet the quality needed to measure the outputs and outcomes of the Virtual reality project?

78. Are the necessary foundations in place to ensure the sustainability of the results of the Virtual reality project?

79. Are you just doing busywork to pass the time?

80. Do the partners have sufficient financial capacity to keep up the benefits produced by the programme?

81. How can you make your needs known?

82. If you are late, will anybody notice?

83. Is the pace of implementing the products of the program ensuring the completeness of the results of the Virtual reality project?

84. Does the program have follow-up mechanisms (to verify the quality of the products, punctuality of delivery, etc.) to measure progress in the achievement of the envisaged results?

85. If task x starts two days late, what is the effect on the Virtual reality project end date?

86. How will you do it?

87. Just how important is your work to the overall success of the Virtual reality project?

88. In what ways can the governance of the Virtual reality project be improved so that it has greater likelihood of achieving future sustainability?

89. What do they need to know about the Virtual reality project?

90. How well did the chosen processes fit the needs of the Virtual reality project?

91. Is your organization showing technical capacity and leadership commitment to keep working with the Virtual reality project and to repeat it?

2.1 Project Management Plan: Virtual reality

92. What if, for example, the positive direction and vision of your organization causes expected trends to change resulting in greater need than expected?

93. What data/reports/tools/etc. do program managers need?

94. What is risk management?

95. Does the implementation plan have an appropriate division of responsibilities?

96. What is the justification?

97. What went right?

98. Is the engineering content at a feasibility level-of-detail, and is it sufficiently complete, to provide an adequate basis for the baseline cost estimate?

99. If the Virtual reality project management plan is a comprehensive document that guides you in Virtual reality project execution and control, then what should it NOT contain?

100. Are the proposed Virtual reality project purposes different than a previously authorized Virtual reality project?

101. Do the proposed changes from the Virtual reality

project include any significant risks to safety?

102. Are cost risk analysis methods applied to develop contingencies for the estimated total Virtual reality project costs?

103. When is the Virtual reality project management plan created?

104. Development trends and opportunities. What if the positive direction and vision of your organization causes expected trends to change?

105. Is the appropriate plan selected based on your organizations objectives and evaluation criteria expressed in Principles and Guidelines policies?

106. Is there anything you would now do differently on your Virtual reality project based on past experience?

107. Is mitigation authorized or recommended?

108. What does management expect of PMs?

109. What are the assumptions?

110. How can you best help your organization to develop consistent practices in Virtual reality project management planning stages?

2.2 Scope Management Plan: Virtual reality

111. Process groups – where do scope management processes fit in?

112. What are the risks that could significantly affect the communication on the Virtual reality project?

113. Deliverables -are the deliverables tangible and verifiable?

114. Does a documented Virtual reality project organizational policy & plan (i.e. governance model) exist?

115. Are post milestone Virtual reality project reviews (PMPR) conducted with your organization at least once a year?

116. Are the payment terms being followed?

117. Are corrective actions and variances reported?

118. Knowing the health of the Virtual reality project – What is the status?

119. Are actuals compared against estimates to analyze and correct variances?

120. Are the quality tools and methods identified in the Quality Plan appropriate to the Virtual reality project?

121. Alignment to strategic goals & objectives?

122. Are there checklists created to demine if all quality processes are followed?

123. Is stakeholder involvement adequate?

124. How do you handle uncertainty or conflict?

125. Are staff skills known and available for each task?

126. Is there a formal process for updating the Virtual reality project baseline?

127. Has stakeholder analysis been conducted, assessing influence on the Virtual reality project and authority levels?

128. What are the Quality Assurance overheads?

129. Time estimation – how much time will be needed?

130. Have the procedures for identifying variances from estimates & adjusting the detailed work program been followed?

2.3 Requirements Management Plan: Virtual reality

131. How will unresolved questions be handled once approval has been obtained?

132. Should you include sub-activities?

133. Is infrastructure setup part of your Virtual reality project?

134. What cost metrics will be used?

135. Is the user satisfied?

136. Define the help desk model. who will take full responsibility?

137. Who came up with this requirement?

138. Is requirements work dependent on any other specific Virtual reality project or non-Virtual reality project activities (e.g. funding, approvals, procurement)?

139. Are actual resource expenditures versus planned still acceptable?

140. How will you develop the schedule of requirements activities?

141. Who will approve the requirements (and if multiple approvers, in what order)?

142. Will you have access to stakeholders when you need them?

143. Which hardware or software, related to, or as outcome of the Virtual reality project is new to your organization?

144. How detailed should the Virtual reality project get?

145. Did you avoid subjective, flowery or non-specific statements?

146. Who will perform the analysis?

147. What is the earliest finish date for this Virtual reality project if it is scheduled to start on ...?

148. Controlling Virtual reality project requirements involves monitoring the status of the Virtual reality project requirements and managing changes to the requirements. Who is responsible for monitoring and tracking the Virtual reality project requirements?

149. Why manage requirements?

150. Will you perform a Requirements Risk assessment and develop a plan to deal with risks?

2.4 Requirements Documentation: Virtual reality

151. How much does requirements engineering cost?

152. The problem with gathering requirements is right there in the word gathering. What images does it conjure?

153. What is a show stopper in the requirements?

154. Validity. does the system provide the functions which best support the customers needs?

155. Who is involved?

156. Do technical resources exist?

157. What kind of entity is a problem ?

158. What is your Elevator Speech?

159. Where are business rules being captured?

160. How will the proposed Virtual reality project help?

161. What is the risk associated with the technology?

162. Is your business case still valid?

163. What are the attributes of a customer?

164. How does what is being described meet the business need?

165. Who is interacting with the system?

166. How does the proposed Virtual reality project contribute to the overall objectives of your organization?

167. How linear / iterative is your Requirements Gathering process (or will it be)?

168. Is the origin of the requirement clearly stated?

169. Does your organization restrict technical alternatives?

170. Verifiability. can the requirements be checked?

2.5 Requirements Traceability Matrix: Virtual reality

171. How small is small enough?

172. Why do you manage scope?

173. What is the WBS?

174. How will it affect the stakeholders personally in career?

175. How do you manage scope?

176. Do you have a clear understanding of all subcontracts in place?

177. What percentage of Virtual reality projects are producing traceability matrices between requirements and other work products?

178. Will you use a Requirements Traceability Matrix?

179. Why use a WBS?

180. What are the chronologies, contingencies, consequences, criteria?

181. Describe the process for approving requirements so they can be added to the traceability matrix and Virtual reality project work can be performed. Will the Virtual reality project requirements become approved in writing?

182. Is there a requirements traceability process in place?

2.6 Project Scope Statement: Virtual reality

183. What is change?

184. Did your Virtual reality project ask for this?

185. Have you been able to thoroughly document the Virtual reality projects assumptions and constraints?

186. Will the risk plan be updated on a regular and frequent basis?

187. Will the risk documents be filed?

188. Elements that deal with providing the detail?

189. Will the qa related information be reported regularly as part of the status reporting mechanisms?

190. If you were to write a list of what should not be included in the scope statement, what are the things that you would recommend be described as out-of-scope?

191. Has the format for tracking and monitoring schedules and costs been defined?

192. Are there issues that could affect the existing requirements for the result, service, or product if the scope changes?

193. What are the possible consequences should a risk

come to occur?

194. Is the plan for Virtual reality project resources adequate?

195. Does the scope statement still need some clarity?

196. Any new risks introduced or old risks impacted. Are there issues that could affect the existing requirements for the result, service, or product if the scope changes?

197. What are the major deliverables of the Virtual reality project?

198. What is the most common tool for helping define the detail?

199. Once its defined, what is the stability of the Virtual reality project scope?

200. Do you anticipate new stakeholders joining the Virtual reality project over time?

201. Is the Virtual reality project sponsor function identified and defined?

202. Is the quality function identified and assigned?

2.7 Assumption and Constraint Log: Virtual reality

203. How can you prevent/fix violations?

204. Are there processes in place to ensure that all the terms and code concepts have been documented consistently?

205. If appropriate, is the deliverable content consistent with current Virtual reality project documents and in compliance with the Document Management Plan?

206. Does the system design reflect the requirements?

207. Contradictory information between document sections?

208. Was the document/deliverable developed per the appropriate or required standards (for example, Institute of Electrical and Electronics Engineers standards)?

209. What strengths do you have?

210. What does an audit system look like?

211. Would known impacts serve as impediments?

212. Does the plan conform to standards?

213. Are you meeting your customers expectations

consistently?

214. Is there adequate stakeholder participation for the vetting of requirements definition, changes and management?

215. Are funding and staffing resource estimates sufficiently detailed and documented for use in planning and tracking the Virtual reality project?

216. Have all stakeholders been identified?

217. What weaknesses do you have?

218. Are there procedures in place to effectively manage interdependencies with other Virtual reality projects / systems?

219. Is the definition of the Virtual reality project scope clear; what needs to be accomplished?

220. Is there a Steering Committee in place?

221. Does the traceability documentation describe the tool and/or mechanism to be used to capture traceability throughout the life cycle?

222. Does a specific action and/or state that is known to violate security policy occur?

2.8 Work Breakdown Structure: Virtual reality

223. What has to be done?

224. Where does it take place?

225. Why would you develop a Work Breakdown Structure?

226. What is the probability of completing the Virtual reality project in less that xx days?

227. How big is a work-package?

228. Do you need another level?

229. Why is it useful?

230. Is it still viable?

231. When does it have to be done?

232. How will you and your Virtual reality project team define the Virtual reality projects scope and work breakdown structure?

233. Who has to do it?

234. How much detail?

235. Can you make it?

236. When do you stop?

237. How far down?

238. When would you develop a Work Breakdown Structure?

239. Is the work breakdown structure (wbs) defined and is the scope of the Virtual reality project clear with assigned deliverable owners?

240. Is it a change in scope?

2.9 WBS Dictionary: Virtual reality

241. Does the scheduling system provide for the identification of work progress against technical and other milestones, and also provide for forecasts of completion dates of scheduled work?

242. Major functional areas of contract effort?

243. Are overhead budgets and costs being handled according to the disclosure statement when applicable, or otherwise properly classified (for example, engineering overhead, IR&D)?

244. Do work packages consist of discrete tasks which are adequately described?

245. Performance to date and material commitment?

246. Actual cost of work performed?

247. What is the end result of a work package?

248. Should you have a test for each code module?

249. Are records maintained to show how management reserves are used?

250. Are indirect costs charged to the appropriate indirect pools and incurring organization?

251. Appropriate work authorization documents which subdivide the contractual effort and responsibilities, within functional organizations?

252. Is budgeted cost for work performed calculated in a manner consistent with the way work is planned?

253. Are direct or indirect cost adjustments being accomplished according to accounting procedures acceptable to us?

254. Does the contractors system description or procedures require that the performance measurement baseline plus management reserve equal the contract budget base?

255. Are the rates for allocating costs from each indirect cost pool to contracts updated as necessary to ensure a realistic monthly allocation of indirect costs without significant year-end adjustments?

256. Are internal budgets for authorized, and not priced changes based on the contractors resource plan for accomplishing the work?

257. Are the requirements for all items of overhead established by rational, traceable processes?

258. Is future work which cannot be planned in detail subdivided to the extent practicable for budgeting and scheduling purposes?

259. Do the lines of authority for incurring indirect costs correspond to the lines of responsibility for management control of the same components of costs?

2.10 Schedule Management Plan: Virtual reality

260. Was the scope definition used in task sequencing?

261. Have all team members been part of identifying risks?

262. Are scheduled deliverables actually delivered?

263. Are the appropriate IT resources adequate to meet planned commitments?

264. Are the results of quality assurance reviews provided to affected groups & individuals?

265. Does the resource management plan include a personnel development plan?

266. Is a pmo (Virtual reality project management office) in place and provide oversight to the Virtual reality project?

267. Are all key components of a Quality Assurance Plan present?

268. Are the activity durations realistic and at an appropriate level of detail for effective management?

269. Perform reality checks on schedules – are all tasks included?

270. Are all vendor contracts closed out?

271. Have all unresolved risks been documented?

272. Were the budget estimates reasonable?

273. Is a process defined for baseline approval and control?

274. Is there an onboarding process in place?

275. Sensitivity analysis?

276. Is the quality assurance team identified?

277. Has the business need been clearly defined?

2.11 Activity List: Virtual reality

278. Is infrastructure setup part of your Virtual reality project?

279. How detailed should a Virtual reality project get?

280. How can the Virtual reality project be displayed graphically to better visualize the activities?

281. What went well?

282. Can you determine the activity that must finish, before this activity can start?

283. In what sequence?

284. How will it be performed?

285. What are you counting on?

286. The wbs is developed as part of a joint planning session. and how do you know that youhave done this right?

287. Who will perform the work?

288. Is there anything planned that does not need to be here?

289. For other activities, how much delay can be tolerated?

290. When do the individual activities need to start

and finish?

291. What is the LF and LS for each activity?

292. What is the total time required to complete the Virtual reality project if no delays occur?

293. Are the required resources available or need to be acquired?

294. What are the critical bottleneck activities?

295. How difficult will it be to do specific activities on this Virtual reality project?

296. When will the work be performed?

2.12 Activity Attributes: Virtual reality

297. How many resources do you need to complete the work scope within a limit of X number of days?

298. How difficult will it be to do specific activities on this Virtual reality project?

299. Is there a trend during the year?

300. Resource is assigned to?

301. Time for overtime?

302. How many days do you need to complete the work scope with a limit of X number of resources?

303. Can you re-assign any activities to another resource to resolve an over-allocation?

304. How difficult will it be to complete specific activities on this Virtual reality project?

305. Are the required resources available?

306. Has management defined a definite timeframe for the turnaround or Virtual reality project window?

307. Why?

308. What is your organizations history in doing similar activities?

309. What is missing?

310. Activity: what is In the Bag?

311. Have you identified the Activity Leveling Priority code value on each activity?

312. Which method produces the more accurate cost assignment?

313. How do you manage time?

314. How much activity detail is required?

2.13 Milestone List: Virtual reality

315. Timescales, deadlines and pressures?

316. Can you derive how soon can the whole Virtual reality project finish?

317. Describe your organizations strengths and core competencies. What factors will make your organization succeed?

318. Competitive advantages?

319. Gaps in capabilities?

320. Vital contracts and partners?

321. Political effects?

322. What background experience, skills, and strengths does the team bring to your organization?

323. Legislative effects?

324. How soon can the activity finish?

325. Level of the Innovation?

326. Who will manage the Virtual reality project on a day-to-day basis?

327. What is the market for your technology, product or service?

328. It is to be a narrative text providing the crucial aspects of your Virtual reality project proposal answering what, who, how, when and where?

329. How late can the activity finish?

330. Effects on core activities, distraction?

331. Sustaining internal capabilities?

2.14 Network Diagram: Virtual reality

332. What are the Major Administrative Issues?

333. How difficult will it be to do specific activities on this Virtual reality project?

334. What activities must follow this activity?

335. If the Virtual reality project network diagram cannot change and you have extra personnel resources, what is the BEST thing to do?

336. Review the logical flow of the network diagram. Take a look at which activities you have first and then sequence the activities. Do they make sense?

337. What controls the start and finish of a job?

338. What are the tools?

339. Are the gantt chart and/or network diagram updated periodically and used to assess the overall Virtual reality project timetable?

340. Can you calculate the confidence level?

341. What job or jobs follow it?

342. Where do you schedule uncertainty time?

343. How confident can you be in your milestone dates and the delivery date?

344. What is the lowest cost to complete this Virtual reality project in xx weeks?

345. If a current contract exists, can you provide the vendor name, contract start, and contract expiration date?

346. What to do and When?

347. Where do schedules come from?

348. Why must you schedule milestones, such as reviews, throughout the Virtual reality project?

349. What can be done concurrently?

2.15 Activity Resource Requirements: Virtual reality

350. Anything else?

351. Organizational Applicability?

352. Why do you do that?

353. How many signatures do you require on a check and does this match what is in your policy and procedures?

354. Are there unresolved issues that need to be addressed?

355. Other support in specific areas?

356. What are constraints that you might find during the Human Resource Planning process?

357. How do you handle petty cash?

358. When does monitoring begin?

359. Do you use tools like decomposition and rolling-wave planning to produce the activity list and other outputs?

360. Which logical relationship does the PDM use most often?

361. What is the Work Plan Standard?

2.16 Resource Breakdown Structure: Virtual reality

362. Changes based on input from stakeholders?

363. Is predictive resource analysis being done?

364. Any changes from stakeholders?

365. What defines a successful Virtual reality project?

366. What is the primary purpose of the human resource plan?

367. Who will use the system?

368. Goals for the Virtual reality project. What is each stakeholders desired outcome for the Virtual reality project?

369. How should the information be delivered?

370. Which resources should be in the resource pool?

371. Who is allowed to perform which functions?

372. Which resource planning tool provides information on resource responsibility and accountability?

373. What is each stakeholders desired outcome for the Virtual reality project?

374. Why is this important?

375. Who will be used as a Virtual reality project team member?

2.17 Activity Duration Estimates: Virtual reality

376. Does a process exist to determine the potential loss or gain if risk events occur?

377. Do procedures exist that identify when and how human resources are introduced and removed from the Virtual reality project?

378. What are the Virtual reality project management deliverables of each process group?

379. How does Virtual reality project integration management relate to the Virtual reality project life cycle, stakeholders, and the other Virtual reality project management knowledge areas?

380. Are activity duration estimates documented?

381. What should be done NEXT?

382. Does the software appear easy to learn?

383. Is a work breakdown structure created to organize and to confirm the scope of each Virtual reality project?

384. How can software assist in Virtual reality project communications?

385. Are Virtual reality project results verified and Virtual reality project documents archived?

386. Do scope statements include the Virtual reality project objectives and expected deliverables?

387. Why is it difficult to use Virtual reality project management software well?

388. Are procedures defined for calculating cost estimates?

389. What is earned value?

390. Consider the changes in the job market for information technology workers. How does the job market and current state of the economy affect human resource management?

391. Which skills do you think are most important for an information technology Virtual reality project manager?

392. Are risks that are likely to affect the Virtual reality project identified and documented?

393. On which process should team members spend the most time?

394. Consider the history of modern quality management. How have experts such as Deming, Juran, Crosby, and Taguchi affected the quality movement and todays use of Six Sigma?

395. Why is outsourcing growing so rapidly?

2.18 Duration Estimating Worksheet: Virtual reality

396. When does your organization expect to be able to complete it?

397. Is this operation cost effective?

398. What is cost and Virtual reality project cost management?

399. What is the total time required to complete the Virtual reality project if no delays occur?

400. Science = process: remember the scientific method?

401. Why estimate time and cost?

402. When, then?

403. What went wrong?

404. What utility impacts are there?

405. What is an Average Virtual reality project?

406. What is next?

407. How should ongoing costs be monitored to try to keep the Virtual reality project within budget?

408. What is your role?

409. Value pocket identification & quantification what are value pockets?

410. Is the Virtual reality project responsive to community need?

411. What work will be included in the Virtual reality project?

2.19 Project Schedule: Virtual reality

412. Why is this particularly bad?

413. Is there a Schedule Management Plan that establishes the criteria and activities for developing, monitoring and controlling the Virtual reality project schedule?

414. Virtual reality project work estimates Who is managing the work estimate quality of work tasks in the Virtual reality project schedule?

415. What is the difference?

416. How can you shorten the schedule?

417. Are activities connected because logic dictates the order in which others occur?

418. Meet requirements?

419. Is the structure for tracking the Virtual reality project schedule well defined and assigned to a specific individual?

420. Are procedures defined by which the Virtual reality project schedule may be changed?

421. Are quality inspections and review activities listed in the Virtual reality project schedule(s)?

422. To what degree is do you feel the entire team was committed to the Virtual reality project schedule?

423. Verify that the update is accurate. Are all remaining durations correct?

424. Why do you need to manage Virtual reality project Risk?

425. Your Virtual reality project management plan results in a Virtual reality project schedule that is too long. If the Virtual reality project network diagram cannot change and you have extra personnel resources, what is the BEST thing to do?

426. How can you fix it?

427. If you can not fix it, how do you do it differently?

428. What is the purpose of a Virtual reality project schedule?

429. Did the Virtual reality project come in under budget?

2.20 Cost Management Plan: Virtual reality

430. Have the reasons why the changes to your organizational systems and capabilities are required?

431. Are Virtual reality project leaders committed to this Virtual reality project full time?

432. Is current scope of the Virtual reality project substantially different than that originally defined?

433. Is it standard practice to formally commit stakeholders to the Virtual reality project via agreements?

434. Are metrics used to evaluate and manage Vendors?

435. Does a documented Virtual reality project organizational policy & plan (i.e. governance model) exist?

436. Were Virtual reality project team members involved in detailed estimating and scheduling?

437. Estimating responsibilities – how will the responsibilities for cost estimating be allocated?

438. Have activity relationships and interdependencies within tasks been adequately identified?

439. Has the Virtual reality project scope been baselined?

440. Who should write the PEP?

441. For cost control purposes?

442. Forecasts – how will the cost to complete the Virtual reality project be forecast?

443. What would you do differently what did not work?

444. Is pert / critical path or equivalent methodology being used?

445. Have all documents been archived in a Virtual reality project repository for each release?

446. Resources – how will human resources be scheduled during each phase of the Virtual reality project?

2.21 Activity Cost Estimates: Virtual reality

447. How do you fund change orders?

448. Were the tasks or work products prepared by the consultant useful?

449. What are you looking for?

450. What makes a good expected result statement?

451. What makes a good activity description?

452. How and when do you enter into Virtual reality project Procurement Management?

453. Were decisions made in a timely manner?

454. What is procurement?

455. Were you satisfied with the work?

456. How difficult will it be to do specific tasks on the Virtual reality project?

457. Was it performed on time?

458. What is Virtual reality project cost management?

459. Why do you manage cost?

460. What is the activity inventory?

461. What were things that you need to improve?

462. The impact and what actions were taken?

463. How do you change activities?

464. Where can you get activity reports?

2.22 Cost Estimating Worksheet: Virtual reality

465. Does the Virtual reality project provide innovative ways for stakeholders to overcome obstacles or deliver better outcomes?

466. Who is best positioned to know and assist in identifying corresponding factors?

467. What costs are to be estimated?

468. What will others want?

469. What is the estimated labor cost today based upon this information?

470. What is the purpose of estimating?

471. Ask: are others positioned to know, are others credible, and will others cooperate?

472. Is the Virtual reality project responsive to community need?

473. What additional Virtual reality project(s) could be initiated as a result of this Virtual reality project?

474. What info is needed?

475. Can a trend be established from historical performance data on the selected measure and are the criteria for using trend analysis or forecasting

methods met?

476. Is it feasible to establish a control group arrangement?

477. Will the Virtual reality project collaborate with the local community and leverage resources?

478. What happens to any remaining funds not used?

479. What can be included?

480. How will the results be shared and to whom?

481. Identify the timeframe necessary to monitor progress and collect data to determine how the selected measure has changed?

2.23 Cost Baseline: Virtual reality

482. Is request in line with priorities?

483. What threats might prevent you from getting there?

484. Have all approved changes to the Virtual reality project requirement been identified and impact on the performance, cost, and schedule baselines documented?

485. Are procedures defined by which the cost baseline may be changed?

486. Have the lessons learned been filed with the Virtual reality project Management Office?

487. Has the Virtual reality projected annual cost to operate and maintain the product(s) or service(s) been approved and funded?

488. Does the suggested change request seem to represent a necessary enhancement to the product?

489. Has the Virtual reality project documentation been archived or otherwise disposed as described in the Virtual reality project communication plan?

490. What is the most important thing to do next to make your Virtual reality project successful?

491. Is the cr within Virtual reality project scope?

492. Have all approved changes to the schedule baseline been identified and impact on the Virtual reality project documented?

493. Will the Virtual reality project fail if the change request is not executed?

494. How fast?

495. Impact to environment?

496. Is there anything unique in this Virtual reality projects scope statement that will affect resources?

497. Review your risk triggers -have your risks changed?

498. Has operations management formally accepted responsibility for operating and maintaining the product(s) or service(s) delivered by the Virtual reality project?

499. Are there contingencies or conditions related to the acceptance?

500. What deliverables come first?

2.24 Quality Management Plan: Virtual reality

501. With the five whys method, the team considers why the issue being explored occurred. do others then take that initial answer and ask why?

502. How does your organization use comparative data and information to improve organizational performance?

503. What are you trying to accomplish?

504. How does your organization manage training and evaluate its effectiveness?

505. Can you perform this task or activity in a more effective manner?

506. Would impacts defined serve as impediments?

507. How do you ensure that your sampling methods and procedures meet your data quality objectives?

508. What would be the next steps or what else should you do at this point?

509. Are there ways to reduce the time it takes to get something approved?

510. Are there trends or hot spots?

511. Can the requirements be traced to the

appropriate components of the solution, as well as test scripts?

512. Why quality management?

513. Have adequate resources been provided by management to ensure Virtual reality project success?

514. What data do you gather/use/compile?

515. What other teams / processes would be impacted by changes to the current process, and how?

516. Were there any deficiencies / issues identified in the prior years self-assessment?

517. How does the material compare to a regulatory threshold?

518. What are your key performance measures/ indicators for tracking progress relative to your action plans?

2.25 Quality Metrics: Virtual reality

519. What is the CMS Benchmark?

520. How are requirements conflicts resolved?

521. How do you communicate results and findings to upper management?

522. Are applicable standards referenced and available?

523. Was the overall quality better or worse than previous products?

524. Where did complaints, returns and warranty claims come from?

525. Which are the right metrics to use?

526. Is a risk containment plan in place?

527. What is the benchmark?

528. Was material distributed on time?

529. Is there a set of procedures to capture, analyze and act on quality metrics?

530. What is the timeline to meet your goal?

531. What level of statistical confidence do you use?

532. Who notifies stakeholders of normal and

abnormal results?

533. When will the Final Guidance will be issued?

534. What metrics do you measure?

535. Are documents on hand to provide explanations of privacy and confidentiality?

536. What if the biggest risk to your business were the already stated people who do not complain?

2.26 Process Improvement Plan: Virtual reality

537. Management commitment at all levels?

538. What personnel are the change agents for your initiative?

539. Have the supporting tools been developed or acquired?

540. Have the frequency of collection and the points in the process where measurements will be made been determined?

541. Purpose of goal: the motive is determined by asking, why do you want to achieve this goal?

542. Have storage and access mechanisms and procedures been determined?

543. Does explicit definition of the measures exist?

544. Has the time line required to move measurement results from the points of collection to databases or users been established?

545. What makes people good SPI coaches?

546. Are there forms and procedures to collect and record the data?

547. Where do you want to be?

548. Are you making progress on the goals?

549. Who should prepare the process improvement action plan?

550. Has a process guide to collect the data been developed?

551. Are you making progress on the improvement framework?

552. What is the return on investment?

553. Why do you want to achieve the goal?

554. What is quality and how will you ensure it?

555. What personnel are the sponsors for that initiative?

2.27 Responsibility Assignment Matrix: Virtual reality

556. What simple tool can you use to help identify and prioritize Virtual reality project risks that is very low tech and high touch?

557. Does the contractor use objective results, design reviews and tests to trace schedule performance?

558. What do people write/say on status/Virtual reality project reports?

559. Do you need to convince people that its well worth the time and effort?

560. Does each role with Accountable responsibility have the authority within your organization to make the required decisions?

561. Evaluate the performance of operating organizations?

562. Ideas for developing soft skills at your organization?

563. Are authorized changes being incorporated in a timely manner?

564. Does the contractors system provide unit or lot costs when applicable?

565. What is the number one predictor of a groups

productivity?

566. Are the overhead pools formally and adequately identified?

567. Contemplated overhead expenditure for each period based on the best information currently available?

568. Are detailed work packages planned as far in advance as practicable?

569. What is the purpose of assigning and documenting responsibility?

570. Identify potential or actual overruns and underruns?

571. What does wbs accomplish?

572. All cwbs elements specified for external reporting?

573. Is work progressively subdivided into detailed work packages as requirements are defined?

2.28 Roles and Responsibilities: Virtual reality

574. Who: who is involved?

575. What expectations were met?

576. Do the values and practices inherent in the culture of your organization foster or hinder the process?

577. What specific behaviors did you observe?

578. Attainable / achievable: the goal is attainable; can you actually accomplish the goal?

579. Was the expectation clearly communicated?

580. Do you take the time to clearly define roles and responsibilities on Virtual reality project tasks?

581. Concern: where are you limited or have no authority, where you can not influence?

582. What is working well?

583. Once the responsibilities are defined for the Virtual reality project, have the deliverables, roles and responsibilities been clearly communicated to every participant?

584. What should you do now to prepare for your career 5+ years from now?

585. How well did the Virtual reality project Team understand the expectations of specific roles and responsibilities?

586. Implementation of actions: Who are the responsible units?

587. What areas of supervision are challenging for you?

588. Does the team have access to and ability to use data analysis tools?

589. Are the quality assurance functions and related roles and responsibilities clearly defined?

590. Required skills, knowledge, experience?

591. Accountabilities: what are the roles and responsibilities of individual team members?

592. Key conclusions and recommendations: Are conclusions and recommendations relevant and acceptable?

2.29 Human Resource Management Plan: Virtual reality

593. Are key risk mitigation strategies added to the Virtual reality project schedule?

594. Are action items captured and managed?

595. Are Virtual reality project leaders committed to this Virtual reality project full time?

596. Are there checklists created to determine if all quality processes are followed?

597. How do you determine what key skills and talents are needed to meet the objectives. Is your organization primarily focused on a specific industry?

598. Is the Virtual reality project schedule available for all Virtual reality project team members to review?

599. Is the current culture aligned with the vision, mission, and values of the department?

600. Are there dependencies with other initiatives or Virtual reality projects?

601. Is there any form of automated support for Issues Management?

602. Virtual reality project definition & scope?

603. Are trade-offs between accepting the risk and

mitigating the risk identified?

604. Are meeting objectives identified for each meeting?

605. Is a payment system in place with proper reviews and approvals?

606. Does the Virtual reality project have a Quality Culture?

607. Do Virtual reality project managers participating in the Virtual reality project know the Virtual reality projects true status first hand?

2.30 Communications Management Plan: Virtual reality

608. Are the stakeholders getting the information others need, are others consulted, are concerns addressed?

609. Are stakeholders internal or external?

610. What to know?

611. What does the stakeholder need from the team?

612. Which stakeholders can influence others?

613. What approaches do you use?

614. What is Virtual reality project communications management?

615. Are there too many who have an interest in some aspect of your work?

616. Who is responsible?

617. Who are the members of the governing body?

618. Are others part of the communications management plan?

619. How is this initiative related to other portfolios, programs, or Virtual reality projects?

620. Timing: when do the effects of the communication take place?

621. Who to share with?

622. Who were proponents/opponents?

623. Which stakeholders are thought leaders, influences, or early adopters?

624. Is the stakeholder role recognized by your organization?

625. Are there common objectives between the team and the stakeholder?

626. How will the person responsible for executing the communication item be notified?

2.31 Risk Management Plan: Virtual reality

627. Is the process being followed?

628. Does the customer have a solid idea of what is required?

629. Are people attending meetings and doing work?

630. Are the metrics meaningful and useful?

631. What would you do differently?

632. Is the customer willing to commit significant time to the requirements gathering process?

633. Internal technical and management reviews?

634. Is the necessary data being captured and is it complete and accurate?

635. Why is product liability a serious issue?

636. Is there additional information that would make you more confident about your analysis?

637. Do you have a consistent repeatable process that is actually used?

638. Are flexibility and reuse paramount?

639. What are some questions that should be

addressed in a risk management plan?

640. How risk averse are you?

641. Risks should be identified during which phase of Virtual reality project management life cycle?

642. Have top software and customer managers formally committed to support the Virtual reality project?

643. Have staff received necessary training?

644. Is the customer willing to participate in reviews?

645. Are tool mentors available?

2.32 Risk Register: Virtual reality

646. Are there any gaps in the evidence?

647. How are risks graded?

648. What is the probability and impact of the risk occurring?

649. What further options might be available for responding to the risk?

650. Are corrective measures implemented as planned?

651. Are there any knock-on effects/impact on any of the other areas?

652. Are implemented controls working as others should?

653. What is a Community Risk Register?

654. What may happen or not go according to plan?

655. What are your key risks/show istoppers and what is being done to manage them?

656. What is the reason for current performance gaps and do the risks and opportunities identified previously account for this?

657. Methodology: how will risk management be performed on this Virtual reality project?

658. What can be done about it?

659. What risks might negatively or positively affect achieving the Virtual reality project objectives?

660. What has changed since the last period?

661. How could corresponding Risk affect the Virtual reality project in terms of cost and schedule?

662. What should the audit role be in establishing a risk management process?

663. What could prevent you delivering on the strategic program objectives and what is being done to mitigate corresponding issues?

664. Why would you develop a risk register?

2.33 Probability and Impact Assessment: Virtual reality

665. Have top software and customer managers formally committed to support the Virtual reality project?

666. How will economic events and trends likely affect the Virtual reality project?

667. Is the customer technically sophisticated in the product area?

668. Which of your Virtual reality projects should be selected when compared with other Virtual reality projects?

669. Workarounds are determined during which step of risk management?

670. What should be the level of coordination?

671. Risk data quality assessment - what is the quality of the data used to determine or assess the risk?

672. Management -what contingency plans do you have if the risk becomes a reality?

673. Are the facilities, expertise, resources, and management know-how available to handle the situation?

674. Does the software engineering team have the

right mix of skills?

675. Is a software Virtual reality project management tool available?

676. How is risk handled within this Virtual reality project organization?

677. Are end-users enthusiastically committed to the Virtual reality project and the system/product to be built?

678. Sensitivity analysis -which risks will have the most impact on the Virtual reality project?

679. How realistic is the timing of introduction?

680. Are testing tools available and suitable?

681. What risks does the employee encounter?

682. Has the need for the Virtual reality project been properly established?

683. What are the chances the event will occur?

2.34 Probability and Impact Matrix: Virtual reality

684. What is the likely future demand of the customer?

685. How well is the risk understood?

686. How would you define a risk?

687. What can possibly go wrong?

688. What action would you take to the identified risks in the Virtual reality project?

689. Are the risk data complete?

690. Is security a central objective?

691. Which is the BEST thing to do?

692. Which role do you have in the Virtual reality project?

693. What things might go wrong?

694. Can it be changed quickly?

695. What things are likely to change?

696. What action do you usually take against risks?

697. Do you have a mechanism for managing change?

2.35 Risk Data Sheet: Virtual reality

698. What are you weak at and therefore need to do better?

699. Potential for recurrence?

700. Whom do you serve (customers)?

701. How do you handle product safely?

702. What do you know?

703. Are new hazards created?

704. Risk of what?

705. What are your core values?

706. Who has a vested interest in how you perform as your organization (our stakeholders)?

707. What is the chance that it will happen?

708. What can happen?

709. What will be the consequences if it happens?

710. If it happens, what are the consequences?

711. What will be the consequences if the risk happens?

712. What are the main opportunities available to you

that you should grab while you can?

713. Has a sensitivity analysis been carried out?

714. What do people affected think about the need for, and practicality of preventive measures?

715. What if client refuses?

716. Do effective diagnostic tests exist?

717. What are you trying to achieve (Objectives)?

2.36 Procurement Management Plan: Virtual reality

718. What areas does the group agree are the biggest success on the Virtual reality project?

719. Are the schedule estimates reasonable given the Virtual reality project?

720. Has the budget been baselined?

721. Is a pmo (Virtual reality project management office) in place which provides oversight to the Virtual reality project?

722. Measurable - are the targets measurable?

723. Is there a procurement management plan in place?

724. Are quality metrics defined?

725. Public engagement – did you get it right?

726. Are all payments made according to the contract(s)?

727. Does a documented Virtual reality project organizational policy & plan (i.e. governance model) exist?

728. How long will it take for the purchase cost to be the same as the lease cost?

729. Is there a formal process for updating the Virtual reality project baseline?

730. Has a quality assurance plan been developed for the Virtual reality project?

731. Are milestone deliverables effectively tracked and compared to Virtual reality project plan?

2.37 Source Selection Criteria: Virtual reality

732. What does a sample rating scale look like?

733. How do you ensure an integrated assessment of proposals?

734. When is it appropriate to issue a Draft Request for Proposal (DRFP)?

735. How are clarifications and communications appropriately used?

736. What common questions or problems are associated with debriefings?

737. Which contract type places the most risk on the seller?

738. Are evaluators ready to begin this task?

739. How should the preproposal conference be conducted?

740. Can you make a cost/technical tradeoff?

741. Who is entitled to a debriefing?

742. Have all evaluators been trained?

743. Who must be notified?

744. Who should attend debriefings?

745. How organization are proposed quotes/prices?

746. How can business terms and conditions be improved to yield more effective price competition?

747. Is a cost realism analysis used?

748. What aspects should the contracting officer brief the Virtual reality project on prior to evaluation of proposals?

749. Can you prevent comparison of proposals?

750. Do you prepare an independent cost estimate?

751. What evidence should be provided regarding proposal evaluations?

2.38 Stakeholder Management Plan: Virtual reality

752. Have all necessary approvals been obtained?

753. Who is accountable for the achievement of the targeted outcome(s) and reports on the progress towards the target?

754. How will you engage this stakeholder and gain commitment?

755. Who is responsible for arranging and managing the review(s)?

756. Have the key elements of a coherent Virtual reality project management strategy been established?

757. How are you doing/what can be done better?

758. Is there an issues management plan in place?

759. Is there a formal process for updating the Virtual reality project baseline?

760. Which of the records created within the Virtual reality project, if any, does the Business Owner require access to?

761. Are the quality tools and methods identified in the Quality Plan appropriate to the Virtual reality project?

762. How accurate and complete is the information?

763. Who will perform the review(s)?

764. Have stakeholder accountabilities & responsibilities been clearly defined?

765. Where to get additional help?

766. Have Virtual reality project success criteria been defined?

767. What has to be purchased?

768. Is the Virtual reality project sponsor clearly communicating the business case or rationale for why this Virtual reality project is needed?

769. How are the overall Virtual reality project development processes to be undertaken to produce the Virtual reality project outputs?

770. Is the amount of effort justified by the anticipated value of forming a new process?

2.39 Change Management Plan: Virtual reality

771. What are the specific target groups/audiences that will be impacted by this change?

772. Who in the business it includes?

773. What processes are in place to manage knowledge about the Virtual reality project?

774. Is there a support model for this application and are the details available for distribution?

775. Who will be the change levers?

776. What prerequisite knowledge do corresponding groups need?

777. What are the training strategies?

778. What relationships will change?

779. What policies and procedures need to be changed?

780. What risks may occur upfront?

781. When does it make sense to customize?

782. How do you know the requirements you documented are the right ones?

783. Do you need a new organization structure?

784. What goal(s) do you hope to accomplish?

785. What new competencies will be required for the roles?

786. Who will do the training?

787. What is the negative impact of communicating too soon or too late?

788. Do you need new systems?

3.0 Executing Process Group: Virtual reality

789. Who are the Virtual reality project stakeholders?

790. What is the difference between using brainstorming and the Delphi technique for risk identification?

791. What is the difference between conceptual, application, and evaluative questions?

792. Mitigate. what will you do to minimize the impact should a risk event occur?

793. Based on your Virtual reality project communication management plan, what worked well?

794. What areas does the group agree are the biggest success on the Virtual reality project?

795. Are the necessary foundations in place to ensure the sustainability of the results of the programme?

796. Do the products created live up to the necessary quality?

797. Were sponsors and decision makers available when needed outside regularly scheduled meetings?

798. How well did the chosen processes fit the needs of the Virtual reality project?

799. How do you control progress of your Virtual reality project?

800. How many different communication channels does the Virtual reality project team have?

801. Who will provide training?

802. What are crucial elements of successful Virtual reality project plan execution?

803. How is Virtual reality project performance information created and distributed?

804. Will new hardware or software be required for servers or client machines?

805. What is in place for ensuring adequate change control on Virtual reality projects that involve outside contracts?

806. What were things that you did well, and could improve, and how?

807. Will a new application be developed using existing hardware, software, and networks?

3.1 Team Member Status Report: Virtual reality

808. How can you make it practical?

809. Are the products of your organizations Virtual reality projects meeting customers objectives?

810. Are the attitudes of staff regarding Virtual reality project work improving?

811. Does your organization have the means (staff, money, contract, etc.) to produce or to acquire the product, good, or service?

812. Will the staff do training or is that done by a third party?

813. Why is it to be done?

814. Is there evidence that staff is taking a more professional approach toward management of your organizations Virtual reality projects?

815. Do you have an Enterprise Virtual reality project Management Office (EPMO)?

816. How does this product, good, or service meet the needs of the Virtual reality project and your organization as a whole?

817. Are your organizations Virtual reality projects more successful over time?

818. Does every department have to have a Virtual reality project Manager on staff?

819. How it is to be done?

820. How much risk is involved?

821. How will resource planning be done?

822. What is to be done?

823. When a teams productivity and success depend on collaboration and the efficient flow of information, what generally fails them?

824. Does the product, good, or service already exist within your organization?

825. What specific interest groups do you have in place?

826. The problem with Reward & Recognition Programs is that the truly deserving people all too often get left out. How can you make it practical?

3.2 Change Request: Virtual reality

827. Describe how modifications, enhancements, defects and/or deficiencies shall be notified (e.g. Problem Reports, Change Requests etc) and managed. Detail warranty and/or maintenance periods?

828. Why control change across the life cycle?

829. Why do you want to have a change control system?

830. What must be taken into consideration when introducing change control programs?

831. How is the change documented (format, content, storage)?

832. How are changes graded and who is responsible for the rating?

833. Has your address changed?

834. Who needs to approve change requests?

835. What are the duties of the change control team?

836. What is a Change Request Form?

837. Who is included in the change control team?

838. Will new change requests be acknowledged in a timely manner?

839. Change request coordination ?

840. Will this change conflict with other requirements changes (e.g., lead to conflicting operational scenarios)?

841. How does your organization control changes before and after software is released to a customer?

842. What has an inspector to inspect and to check?

843. Has a formal technical review been conducted to assess technical correctness?

844. What needs to be communicated?

845. Who can suggest changes?

846. How many lines of code must be changed to implement the change?

3.3 Change Log: Virtual reality

847. Does the suggested change request represent a desired enhancement to the products functionality?

848. Is the change request within Virtual reality project scope?

849. Is the submitted change a new change or a modification of a previously approved change?

850. When was the request approved?

851. Who initiated the change request?

852. Is the change backward compatible without limitations?

853. When was the request submitted?

854. Where do changes come from?

855. How does this relate to the standards developed for specific business processes?

856. How does this change affect the timeline of the schedule?

857. Do the described changes impact on the integrity or security of the system?

858. How does this change affect scope?

859. Will the Virtual reality project fail if the change

request is not executed?

860. Is the change request open, closed or pending?

861. Is the requested change request a result of changes in other Virtual reality project(s)?

862. Is this a mandatory replacement?

863. Should a more thorough impact analysis be conducted?

3.4 Decision Log: Virtual reality

864. What are the cost implications?

865. With whom was the decision shared or considered?

866. How consolidated and comprehensive a story can you tell by capturing currently available incident data in a central location and through a log of key decisions during an incident?

867. Which variables make a critical difference?

868. How do you define success?

869. What is the line where eDiscovery ends and document review begins?

870. At what point in time does loss become unacceptable?

871. How does provision of information, both in terms of content and presentation, influence acceptance of alternative strategies?

872. How do you know when you are achieving it?

873. What makes you different or better than others companies selling the same thing?

874. Decision-making process; how will the team make decisions?

875. Behaviors; what are guidelines that the team has identified that will assist them with getting the most out of team meetings?

876. What is your overall strategy for quality control / quality assurance procedures?

877. How does an increasing emphasis on cost containment influence the strategies and tactics used?

878. Who is the decisionmaker?

879. Adversarial environment. is your opponent open to a non-traditional workflow, or will it likely challenge anything you do?

880. What is the average size of your matters in an applicable measurement?

881. It becomes critical to track and periodically revisit both operational effectiveness; Are you noticing all that you need to, and are you interpreting what you see effectively?

882. Does anything need to be adjusted?

883. Do strategies and tactics aimed at less than full control reduce the costs of management or simply shift the cost burden?

3.5 Quality Audit: Virtual reality

884. Are all staff empowered and encouraged to contribute to ongoing improvement efforts?

885. How is the Strategic Plan (and other plans) reviewed and revised?

886. How does your organization know that its research funding systems are appropriately effective and constructive in enabling quality research outcomes?

887. What does the organizarion look for in a Quality audit?

888. How does your organization know that its range of activities are being reviewed as rigorously and constructively as they could be?

889. What will the Observer get to Observe?

890. How does your organization know that its system for ensuring that its training activities are appropriately resourced and support is appropriately effective and constructive?

891. How does your organization know that its policy management system is appropriately effective and constructive?

892. For each device to be reconditioned, are device specifications, such as appropriate engineering drawings, component specifications and software

specifications, maintained?

893. Does the supplier use a formal quality system?

894. How does your organization know that the review processes are effective?

895. How does your organization know that its relationships with other relevant organizations are appropriately effective and constructive?

896. How does your organization know that its system for attending to the health and wellbeing of its staff is appropriately effective and constructive?

897. How does your organization know that its processes for managing severance are appropriately effective, constructive and fair?

898. Is refuse and garbage adequately stored and disposed of with sufficient frequency to prevent contamination?

899. How does your organization know that its Mission, Vision and Values Statements are appropriate and effectively guiding your organization?

900. How does your organization know that its security arrangements are appropriately effective and constructive?

901. How does your organization know that its system for ensuring a positive organizational climate is appropriately effective and constructive?

902. Are goals well supported with strategies,

operational plans, manuals and training?

903. How does your organization know that its advisory services are appropriately effective and constructive?

3.6 Team Directory: Virtual reality

904. Who will be the stakeholders on your next Virtual reality project?

905. Who will write the meeting minutes and distribute?

906. Who will talk to the customer?

907. Where will the product be used and/or delivered or built when appropriate?

908. Contract requirements complied with?

909. How do unidentified risks impact the outcome of the Virtual reality project?

910. Who should receive information (all stakeholders)?

911. Who will report Virtual reality project status to all stakeholders?

912. How does the team resolve conflicts and ensure tasks are completed?

913. How will you accomplish and manage the objectives?

914. Process decisions: which organizational elements and which individuals will be assigned management functions?

915. When does information need to be distributed?

916. Process decisions: are contractors adequately prosecuting the work?

917. Does a Virtual reality project team directory list all resources assigned to the Virtual reality project?

918. Process decisions: how well was task order work performed?

919. How and in what format should information be presented?

920. When will you produce deliverables?

921. Do purchase specifications and configurations match requirements?

3.7 Team Operating Agreement: Virtual reality

922. How will your group handle planned absences?

923. Do you leverage technology engagement tools group chat, polls, screen sharing, etc.?

924. Do you ensure that all participants know how to use the required technology?

925. Do you record meetings for the already stated unable to attend?

926. Do you brief absent members after they view meeting notes or listen to a recording?

927. What are the boundaries (organizational or geographic) within which you operate?

928. How will you divide work equitably?

929. Do you send out the agenda and meeting materials in advance?

930. Must your team members rely on the expertise of other members to complete tasks?

931. How do you want to be thought of and known within your organization?

932. Did you prepare participants for the next meeting?

933. What administrative supports will be put in place to support the team and the teams supervisor?

934. To whom do you deliver your services?

935. Do you post any action items, due dates, and responsibilities on the team website?

936. Is compensation based on team and individual performance?

937. Reimbursements: how will the team members be reimbursed for expenses and time commitments?

938. Are there more than two native languages represented by your team?

939. Do you begin with a question to engage everyone?

940. What is the number of cases currently teamed?

3.8 Team Performance Assessment: Virtual reality

941. Lack of method variance in self-reported affect and perceptions at work: Reality or artifact?

942. How do you manage human resources?

943. To what degree do team members understand one anothers roles and skills?

944. How hard did you try to make a good selection?

945. To what degree are the goals realistic?

946. To what degree are the goals ambitious?

947. To what degree do team members feel that the purpose of the team is important, if not exciting?

948. What structural changes have you made or are you preparing to make?

949. To what degree can all members engage in open and interactive considerations?

950. To what degree are the teams goals and objectives clear, simple, and measurable?

951. To what degree do members understand and articulate the same purpose without relying on ambiguous abstractions?

952. How does Virtual reality project termination impact Virtual reality project team members?

953. To what degree does the teams work approach provide opportunity for members to engage in fact-based problem solving?

954. To what degree can team members frequently and easily communicate with one another?

955. To what degree will new and supplemental skills be introduced as the need is recognized?

956. Do you give group members authority to make at least some important decisions?

957. To what degree does the teams purpose contain themes that are particularly meaningful and memorable?

958. To what degree does the teams work approach provide opportunity for members to engage in results-based evaluation?

959. To what degree does the team possess adequate membership to achieve its ends?

960. How hard do you try to make a good selection?

3.9 Team Member Performance Assessment: Virtual reality

961. Why were corresponding selected?

962. Are any validation activities performed?

963. What stakeholders must be involved in the development and oversight of the performance plan?

964. How do you use data to inform instruction and improve staff achievement?

965. What are best practices for delivering and developing training evaluations to maximize the benefits of leveraging emerging technologies?

966. Is there reluctance to join a team?

967. What are the key duties or tasks of the Ratee?

968. How are evaluation results utilized?

969. What is the large, desired outcome?

970. What future plans (e.g., modifications) do you have for your program?

971. Does statute or regulation require the job responsibility?

972. What are the standards or expectations for success?

973. What types of learning are targeted (e.g., cognitive, affective, psychomotor, procedural)?

974. What were the challenges that resulted for training and assessment?

975. What are the staffs preferences for training on technology-based platforms?

976. How is the timing of assessments organized (e.g., pre/post-test, single point during training, multiple reassessment during training)?

977. How will you identify your Team Leaders?

978. What tools are available to determine whether all contract functional and compliance areas of performance objectives, measures, and incentives have been met?

3.10 Issue Log: Virtual reality

979. Who have you worked with in past, similar initiatives?

980. Are there potential barriers between the team and the stakeholder?

981. Which team member will work with each stakeholder?

982. Are the stakeholders getting the information they need, are they consulted, are concerns addressed?

983. Can you think of other people who might have concerns or interests?

984. Are the Virtual reality project issues uniquely identified, including to which product they refer?

985. Can an impact cause deviation beyond team, stage or Virtual reality project tolerances?

986. Who do you turn to if you have questions?

987. What is the stakeholders political influence?

988. What is the impact on the risks?

989. Why do you manage human resources?

990. How much time does it take to do it?

991. What approaches to you feel are the best ones to use?

992. Is access to the Issue Log controlled?

993. Who reported the issue?

4.0 Monitoring and Controlling Process Group: Virtual reality

994. How is agile portfolio management done?

995. Is the schedule for the set products being met?

996. What are the deliverables?

997. In what way has the program come up with innovative measures for problem-solving?

998. Did the Virtual reality project team have the right skills?

999. If action is called for, what form should it take?

1000. Is it what was agreed upon?

1001. Contingency planning. if a risk event occurs, what will you do?

1002. Is there sufficient funding available for this?

1003. Feasibility: how much money, time, and effort can you put into this?

1004. Is the program making progress in helping to achieve the set results?

1005. What business situation is being addressed?

1006. Just how important is your work to the overall

success of the Virtual reality project?

4.1 Project Performance Report: Virtual reality

1007. To what degree can the cognitive capacity of individuals accommodate the flow of information?

1008. To what degree will each member have the opportunity to advance his or her professional skills in all three of the above categories while contributing to the accomplishment of the teams purpose and goals?

1009. To what degree do team members frequently explore the teams purpose and its implications?

1010. To what degree does the task meet individual needs?

1011. To what degree do members articulate the goals beyond the team membership?

1012. To what degree are the members clear on what they are individually responsible for and what they are jointly responsible for?

1013. To what degree does the funding match the requirement?

1014. To what degree will the team adopt a concrete, clearly understood, and agreed-upon approach that will result in achievement of the teams goals?

1015. To what degree does the information network communicate information relevant to the task?

1016. To what degree can team members vigorously define the teams purpose in considerations with others who are not part of the functioning team?

1017. How is the data used?

1018. To what degree does the formal organization make use of individual resources and meet individual needs?

1019. To what degree are fresh input and perspectives systematically caught and added (for example, through information and analysis, new members, and senior sponsors)?

1020. To what degree is the team cognizant of small wins to be celebrated along the way?

1021. To what degree can team members meet frequently enough to accomplish the teams ends?

1022. What is the PRS?

1023. What is in it for you?

1024. To what degree does the informal organization make use of individual resources and meet individual needs?

1025. To what degree do the structures of the formal organization motivate taskrelevant behavior and facilitate task completion?

4.2 Variance Analysis: Virtual reality

1026. There are detailed schedules which support control account and work package start and completion dates/events?

1027. Do you identify potential or actual budget-based and time-based schedule variances?

1028. How does the monthly budget compare to the actual experience?

1029. Is the anticipated (firm and potential) business base Virtual reality projected in a rational, consistent manner?

1030. Are overhead cost budgets established for each department which has authority to incur overhead costs?

1031. What can be the cause of an increase in costs?

1032. How do you identify potential or actual overruns and underruns?

1033. Are significant decision points, constraints, and interfaces identified as key milestones?

1034. Can the contractor substantiate work package and planning package budgets?

1035. Are there changes in the overhead pool and/or organization structures?

1036. How do you identify and isolate causes of favorable and unfavorable cost and schedule variances?

1037. Are overhead costs budgets established on a basis consistent with the anticipated direct business base?

1038. How have the setting and use of standards changed over time?

1039. How are material, labor, and overhead variances calculated and recorded?

1040. How do you evaluate the impact of schedule changes, work around, et?

1041. Is cost and schedule performance measurement done in a consistent, systematic manner?

1042. Is the entire contract planned in time-phased control accounts to the extent practicable?

4.3 Earned Value Status: Virtual reality

1043. When is it going to finish?

1044. Where Is evidence-based earned value in your organization reported?

1045. If earned value management (EVM) is so good in determining the true status of a Virtual reality project and Virtual reality project its completion, why is it that hardly any one uses it in information systems related Virtual reality projects?

1046. Are you hitting your Virtual reality projects targets?

1047. What is the unit of forecast value?

1048. Validation is a process of ensuring that the developed system will actually achieve the stakeholders desired outcomes; Are you building the right product? What do you validate?

1049. How much is it going to cost by the finish?

1050. Where are your problem areas?

1051. Verification is a process of ensuring that the developed system satisfies the stakeholders agreements and specifications; Are you building the product right? What do you verify?

1052. Earned value can be used in almost any Virtual reality project situation and in almost any Virtual reality project environment. it may be used on large Virtual reality projects, medium sized Virtual reality projects, tiny Virtual reality projects (in cut-down form), complex and simple Virtual reality projects and in any market sector. some people, of course, know all about earned value, they have used it for years - but perhaps not as effectively as they could have?

1053. How does this compare with other Virtual reality projects?

4.4 Risk Audit: Virtual reality

1054. Do industry specialists and business risk auditors enhance audit reporting accuracy?

1055. Has risk management been considered when planning an event?

1056. Will an appropriate standard of care be applied to all involved?

1057. Where will the next scandal or adverse media involving your organization come from?

1058. How effective are your risk controls?

1059. Do you conduct risk assessments on all programs, activities and events?

1060. Are corresponding safety and risk management policies posted for all to see?

1061. Are tools for analysis and design available?

1062. Do you meet the legislative requirements (for example PAYG, super contributions) for paid employees?

1063. What are the commonly used work arounds in high risk areas?

1064. What is happening in other jurisdictions? Could that happen here?

1065. Should additional substantive testing be conducted because of the risk audit results?

1066. Are your rules, by-laws and practices non-discriminatory?

1067. Is all required equipment available?

1068. Has an event time line been developed?

1069. If applicable; are compilers and code generators available and suitable for the product to be built?

1070. Is your organization able to present documentary evidence in support of compliance?

1071. Are all participants informed of safety issues?

1072. To what extent should analytical procedures be utilized in the risk-assessment process?

1073. Does your board meet regularly and document all decisions and actions?

4.5 Contractor Status Report: Virtual reality

1074. What was the budget or estimated cost for your organizations services?

1075. What process manages the contracts?

1076. Who can list a Virtual reality project as organization experience, your organization or a previous employee of your organization?

1077. If applicable; describe your standard schedule for new software version releases. Are new software version releases included in the standard maintenance plan?

1078. How is risk transferred?

1079. What are the minimum and optimal bandwidth requirements for the proposed solution?

1080. How does the proposed individual meet each requirement?

1081. What was the actual budget or estimated cost for your organizations services?

1082. Are there contractual transfer concerns?

1083. What was the final actual cost?

1084. How long have you been using the services?

1085. What was the overall budget or estimated cost?

1086. What is the average response time for answering a support call?

1087. Describe how often regular updates are made to the proposed solution. Are corresponding regular updates included in the standard maintenance plan?

4.6 Formal Acceptance: Virtual reality

1088. Who would use it?

1089. What is the Acceptance Management Process?

1090. How does your team plan to obtain formal acceptance on your Virtual reality project?

1091. General estimate of the costs and times to complete the Virtual reality project?

1092. What function(s) does it fill or meet?

1093. Does it do what Virtual reality project team said it would?

1094. What are the requirements against which to test, Who will execute?

1095. What lessons were learned about your Virtual reality project management methodology?

1096. Who supplies data?

1097. What features, practices, and processes proved to be strengths or weaknesses?

1098. Was the Virtual reality project managed well?

1099. Have all comments been addressed?

1100. Was the Virtual reality project goal achieved?

1101. Did the Virtual reality project manager and team act in a professional and ethical manner?

1102. Was the client satisfied with the Virtual reality project results?

1103. Was the sponsor/customer satisfied?

1104. What was done right?

1105. Do you buy pre-configured systems or build your own configuration?

1106. Was business value realized?

1107. How well did the team follow the methodology?

5.0 Closing Process Group: Virtual reality

1108. What is an Encumbrance?

1109. What can you do better next time, and what specific actions can you take to improve?

1110. Was the user/client satisfied with the end product?

1111. What is the overall risk of the Virtual reality project to your organization?

1112. What is the risk of failure to your organization?

1113. Did you do things well?

1114. What areas does the group agree are the biggest success on the Virtual reality project?

1115. Can the lesson learned be replicated?

1116. Were risks identified and mitigated?

1117. What could be done to improve the process?

1118. Did the Virtual reality project team have enough people to execute the Virtual reality project plan?

1119. Are there funding or time constraints?

1120. When will the Virtual reality project be done?

1121. What were things that you did very well and want to do the same again on the next Virtual reality project?

1122. What areas were overlooked on this Virtual reality project?

5.1 Procurement Audit: Virtual reality

1123. Are there policies regarding special approval for capital expenditures?

1124. Does the procurement function/unit have the ability to negotiate with customers and suppliers?

1125. Which contracts have been awarded for works, supply of products or provision of services?

1126. Are purchase requisitions used to generate purchase orders?

1127. Has your organization taken a well-grounded decision about the procurement procedure chosen and has it documented the process?

1128. Is the issuance of purchase orders scheduled so that orders are not issued daily?

1129. Are there mechanisms in place to evaluate the performance of the departments suppliers?

1130. Is there no evidence that the expert has influenced the decisions taken by the public authority in his/her interest or in the interest of a specific contractor?

1131. Are there procedures to ensure that changes to purchase orders will be updated on the computer files?

1132. Is there any objection?

1133. Which are necessary components of a financial audit report under the Single Audit Act?

1134. How do you address the risk of fraud and corruption?

1135. Are controls proportionated to risks?

1136. Are regulations and protective measures in place to avoid corruption?

1137. Does the strategy ensure that needs are met, and not exceeded?

1138. Is there no evidence of favouritism towards a particular contractor during the evaluation and negotiation processes?

1139. Are services/tasks combined in such a way that the market is used where relevant?

1140. Are required quality and service standards set?

1141. Are criteria and sub-criteria set suitable to identify the tender that offers best value for money?

1142. Does the procurement Virtual reality project have a clear goal and does the goal meet the specified needs of the users?

5.2 Contract Close-Out: Virtual reality

1143. Parties: who is involved?

1144. How/when used ?

1145. Has each contract been audited to verify acceptance and delivery?

1146. Was the contract complete without requiring numerous changes and revisions?

1147. Change in attitude or behavior?

1148. Was the contract type appropriate?

1149. What is capture management?

1150. Have all contracts been closed?

1151. Parties: Authorized?

1152. Have all contract records been included in the Virtual reality project archives?

1153. Was the contract sufficiently clear so as not to result in numerous disputes and misunderstandings?

1154. How does it work?

1155. Change in knowledge?

1156. Change in circumstances?

1157. Are the signers the authorized officials?

1158. What happens to the recipient of services?

1159. Have all acceptance criteria been met prior to final payment to contractors?

1160. Have all contracts been completed?

1161. How is the contracting office notified of the automatic contract close-out?

5.3 Project or Phase Close-Out: Virtual reality

1162. Which changes might a stakeholder be required to make as a result of the Virtual reality project?

1163. In addition to assessing whether the Virtual reality project was successful, it is equally critical to analyze why it was or was not fully successful. Are you including this?

1164. Complete yes or no?

1165. When and how were information needs best met?

1166. What was learned?

1167. What could have been improved?

1168. What is the information level of detail required for each stakeholder?

1169. What are the informational communication needs for each stakeholder?

1170. What was expected from each stakeholder?

1171. What benefits or impacts does the stakeholder group expect to obtain as a result of the Virtual reality project?

1172. Who is responsible for award close-out?

1173. What security considerations needed to be addressed during the procurement life cycle?

1174. What are the marketing communication needs for each stakeholder?

1175. Is the lesson significant, valid, and applicable?

1176. What advantages do the an individual interview have over a group meeting, and vice-versa?

1177. Who exerted influence that has positively affected or negatively impacted the Virtual reality project?

5.4 Lessons Learned: Virtual reality

1178. What did you put in place to ensure success?

1179. What is the economic growth rate?

1180. What is your working hypothesis, if you have one?

1181. How effectively and timely was your organizational change impact identified and planned for?

1182. What is your organizational ideology?

1183. What are the Benefits of Measurements?

1184. What on the Virtual reality project worked well and was effective in the delivery of the product?

1185. How useful was your testing?

1186. What are the conceptual limits of the research?

1187. How to write up the lesson identified – how will you document the results of your analysis corresponding that you have an li ready to take the next step in the ll process?

1188. Is your organization willing to expose problems or mistakes for the betterment of the collective whole, and can you do this in a way that does not intimidate employees or workers?

1189. How effective were Best Practices & Lessons Learned from prior Virtual reality projects utilized in this Virtual reality project?

1190. What were the key issues?

1191. How effective was the support you received during implementation of the product/service?

1192. What is the quality and content of communication?

1193. How will you allocate your funding resources?

1194. How effective was the quality assurance process?

1195. What were the major enablers to a quick response?

1196. Did the team work well together?

1197. How mature are the observations?

Index

CPSIA information can be obtained
at www.ICGtesting.com
Printed in the USA
BVHW061630260619
552031BV00011B/423/P

9 780655 549611